GRADUATING TO THE 9-5 WORLD

Dedicated to

To my parents "Big" Joe and Sheila for the past 28 years of support and love. Without their examples of determination and love, I would have never accomplished any of my goals.

To my lovely wife, Rose, my sisters Kelly and Megan, my brother Mike, and my best friend Rupp for all their patience and endurance while I endlessly talked about the importance of putting the subject of this book into print.

GRADUATING TO THE 9-5 WORLD

Jerry Bouchard

WITHDRAWN

IMPACT PUBLICATIONS
Woodbridge, VA

GRADUATING TO THE 9-5 WORLD

Copyright © 1991 by Jerry Bouchard

All rights reserved. Printed in the United States of America. No part of this book may be used or reproduced in any manner whatsoever without written permission of the publisher: IMPACT PUBLICATIONS, 4580 Sunshine Court, Woodbridge, VA 22192.

Library of Congress Cataloging-in-Publication Data

Bouchard, Jerry, 1962-
    Graduating to the 9-5 world / Jerry Bouchard.
        p. cm.
    Includes index.
    ISBN 0-942710-50-9 : $11.95.
      1. Job hunting—United States. 2. College graduates—Employment—United States. 3. Employment interviewing—United States. 4. Employee orientation. I. Title.
HF5382.75.U6B68   1991
650.14—dc20   91-17320
                                                              CIP

Cover designed by ABS Graphics, 8564 Custer Court, Manassas, VA 22111, Tel. 703/361-7415

For information on distribution or quantity discount rates, call (703/361-7300), FAX (703/335-9486), or write to: Sales Department, IMPACT PUBLICATIONS, 4580 Sunshine Court, Woodbridge, VA 22192. Distributed to the trade by National Book Network, 4720 Boston Way, Suite A, Lanham, MD 20706, Tel. 301/459-8696.

CONTENTS

ACKNOWLEDGEMENTS v
PREFACE vii

1 SO YOU HAVE A COLLEGE DEGREE 1

2 UNDERSTANDING THE 9-5 WORLD 18

3 PLOTTING YOUR COURSE 33

4 ORGANIZING YOUR
JOB SEARCH STRATEGY 52

5 THE INTERVIEW 78

6 THE FIRST 90 DAYS—
10 Commandments For the Rookie 9-5er 102

7 UNCERTAINTY IS A CERTAINTY 127

8 REAL WORLD SHOCKS
OUTSIDE THE WORKPLACE 156

9 THE OTHER SIDE:
Successful and Happy 175

INDEX 183

ACKNOWLEDGEMENTS

I would like to thank all those individuals, scattered throughout the country, who openly discussed their feelings with me about their dilemmas, concerns, and personal experiences. Without their candid observations, the following pages would not have been possible.

I wish to express special gratitude to those college administrators and business executives who graciously assisted me on numerous occasions. And for those of you who revealed *"off the record"* opinions about various issues, I want to thank you, in advance, on behalf of the readers. Your shared experiences will allow them an opportunity to better understand some of the confusing situations they may face as they embrace the 9-5 world of work.

Without doubt, I owe a great deal to my editors and mentors (Jim Killingsworth) who helped me develop my ideas and writing into a feasible manuscript. I cannot convey how valuable Jan Booker, my final editor, was to this entire project. Jan, thank you a million times over!

And to all those who agreed that the following pages are topics which needed to be addressed in a different perspective, I hope this book helps.

PREFACE

Wouldn't it be nice each time you passed a test if you received credit towards the next one? Unfortunately, your performance on past exams is given no consideration towards future challenges. Entering the 9-5 world is very similar—all your past performance, in the college curriculum, the athletic arena, or even graduate school, is not recognized as credit, but rather as an indicator that you should be given a chance to take the *"9-5 test."*

Approximately five years ago I was sitting at a Washington, DC bar Happy Hour listening to a group of recent college grads complain how the adjustment into the 9-5 workplace was very cruel and unfair. Immediately I laughed thinking that they must have gone to the wrong school or majored in the wrong curriculum. Soon I discovered that group of people were from UCLA, Marquette, Princeton, Georgetown as well as Lynchburg College, Stephen Austin, Northern Virginia Community College, and Memphis State. Furthermore, this group held as diversified an assortment of degrees (education, business, law, medicine, biology) as the variety of schools they attended. This informal Friday afternoon gathering eventually evolved into an all night debate against the system. At that time, I too did not understand what was the so-called *"system."* The system, although none of us defined it, would eventually be revealed to me as *"anybody or anything that affected the transition of a new 9-5er into the workplace."*

Throughout the night, many of the group suggested various books that might help someone enduring the same difficulties. It was, however, always agreed that the books were helpful, but greatly lacking in directly addressing *"our"* problems. After the tenth *"if only someone would have told me"* complaint, I agreed that the system was clearly lacking for so many new 9-5ers, with such varied backgrounds, to be having the same problem. The discussion continued until about 11:30pm, when we all realized that if we missed the subway it would be a long walk home. Upon saying goodnight, one of the girls said, *"we should write a book and tell new grads what really to expect so they won't be so shocked at what awaits them."*

Although that statement meant very little to me at the time, it would become a project that eventually took me to campuses all over the country, to businesses of all sizes, and even psychiatrists to try and find out why it is

- that some employers refuse to hire new college graduates no matter what their qualifications.

- that being a new 9-5er allows one to have a large buffer zone for errors.

- that a 35¢ an hour raise might be better than a $1000 a year salary raise.

- that some employers will refuse to hire based on one's personal habits and beliefs.

- that veteran 9-5ers consider college grads to be the biggest threat to their personal well being and will do anything to cause them problems.

- that many employers ask hundreds of illegal questions during their interviews.

Preface

- that some employers will cheat, lie, and steal to get business and expect new 9-5ers to accept this standard of behavior.

- that moving back in with one's parents can be mentally destructive for all parties involved.

- that most must adjust from 5 months vacation a year to 5 days a year.

- that there is a very good chance that you will never use one bit of your major field of study after you walk off the graduation stage.

- that car dealers will sell you a car with the hope you will miss payment, knowing that you can't afford it, so that they may repossess it.

- that some college administrators feel that college does a poor job in preparing new grads for the real world.

- that veteran 9-5ers feel they could greatly assist any new grad, but hesitate since no one helped them when they entered the job market.

- that many new grads described the adjustment into the 9-5 workplace as the worst year of their life. Some even admitted their drug/alcohol addiction was a result of not being prepared.

Shocking, isn't it? It is sad to say, but that is only the tip of the iceberg. *Graduating To the 9-5 World* is unique because it is written from both sides of the fence. Many of the individuals who contributed were new graduates who were experiencing this turmoil. Likewise, many employers revealed the hows and whys to this difficult transition. This book does not instruct you how to construct the perfect resume, or how to shake hands with your interviewer. The following are pages of information that thousands of new 9-

5ers, veteran 9-5ers, college administrators, and employers noted as being the most important issues that were being incorrectly or insufficiently addressed.

The 9-5 world can take it's toll on many of its participants. However, this need not happen to you. As the following pages outline, you can be a step ahead by better knowing what is on the *"9-5 test"!*

Chapter One

SO YOU HAVE A COLLEGE DEGREE

Isn't it great to be finished with college? Now you can go out into the world to make money and enjoy the good life. But wouldn't it be nice to have *Cliff Notes* or some other blueprint for this next chapter of your life?

While most recent college grads consciously think they understand the adjustments awaiting them in the 9-5 culture, the reality rarely fails to be a shocker. Despite four years of learning, living, and surviving on your own, the law of the workplace is often *"age before brains."* Entering the 9-5 culture means going through some personal lifestyle adjustments; it also requires adapting to a new and, in many ways, foreign environment. Being the *"green kid"* on the block, you will have to reestablish yourself. Until you demonstrate on-the-job accomplishments to your new employer, you might once again become a freshman.

FACING THE 9-5 SHOCK

It's difficult to pinpoint exactly why the 9-5 shock occurs. For one thing, the so-called 9-5 shock can manifest itself in so many different ways. However, at the heart of the matter, most difficulties experienced by recent graduates are in some way related to a discrepancy between expectations and reality—how you hoped it would be versus how it really is. Maybe you didn't really begin to speculate about life after college until graduation was upon you. The truth is, no matter how much you attempted to discern what would be awaiting you as a newcomer on the 9-5 scene, your ability to accurately anticipate the nature of the approaching transition will be significantly hindered by a lack of prior exposure. Your expectations will be further marred by any assumption that work could not really be so different from school. The 9-5 shock occurs because, while college may prepare students academically, there are innumerable practical considerations which college will not prepare you for.

There are innumerable practical considerations which college will not prepare you for.

This book is designed to encourage you to look ahead and to correct some naive expectations which may hold the seeds for your own 9-5 shock. Some of your false expectations and impressions may not be entirely conscious. You may simply have failed to anticipate some highly relevant factors which will influence your assimilation into the working life. ***Graduating to the 9-5 World*** is aimed at facilitating the college student or recent graduate's ability to think about and prepare for some aspects of the 9-5 life which are rarely touched upon in the classroom. It assumes that an individual will adjust more quickly to a transition when he or she is mentally prepared for it. Blind expectations should be replaced with awareness and farsightedness. This book will allow you to identify the added insights and tools which you will need to make your degree work for you.

It is important to anticipate all of the possibilities. You will not encounter all of the frustrations discussed in this book. Nevertheless, you will definitely experience some aspect of the 9-5 shock. Worst-case scenario planning prepares you for the worst and leaves you much to be thankful for when you find that many of the calamities you anticipated pass you by.

> *Your degree will pay off, but not without continued effort on your part.*

In college, your vision rarely extends past each pending short-term goal. College students are not encouraged to do much realistic visualizing past graduation day. You know that you will graduate. You should expect to find a desirable job. You would not invest so much time, money, and effort into college if you did not expect it to pay off royally and more or less immediately. Perhaps the biggest pill you will have to swallow in adjusting to the 9-5 shock will be ridding yourself of the expectation of quick and easy pay backs upon attaining your degree. Your degree will pay off, but not without continued effort on your part.

TRANSFERABLE COLLEGE SKILLS

Doesn't the discipline required to attain a degree serve a graduate equally well in the job market? Yes, it does. But discipline only goes so far and it is not enough. Dr. Victor

Lindquist, director of the Northwestern University Placement Center and author of the annual *Lindquist-Endicott Report* on employment trends for college graduates explains, *"anyone who argues that the college environment is a realistic representation of the work environment is talking a bunch of nonsense."* Dr. Lindquist unequivocally supports the need of a college diploma, but agrees that the application of that diploma to real life situations is not always simple.

Several college campus recruiters voiced their opinions about new graduates' perception of the workplace. They all indicated that students need to understand that the degree is only *"a starting point."*

Listen to Peter, a 1987 graduate:

> *"I felt sure that my diploma, 20 resumes to different companies, and good references would net me $20,000 a year! I laugh or maybe cry at my ignorance. Many of my friends felt the same way."*

For four years or more, the college world consisted of such projects as solving a steel company's financial woes, hypothesizing which drugs the FDA should develop to fight AIDS, or mapping a strategy to thwart a computer virus infecting the Pentagon. After such glorified pseudo-real-world applications of knowledge, high hopes and vivid dreams are only natural. You might wish you were having a dream when your first duties include making coffee, running the fax machine and watching others make the big deals.

A diploma, however, is no more than a passing grade. You're kidding yourself if you to think that jobs and happiness automatically follow graduation.

PREPARATION FOR LIFE

Aren't four years of intensive study more than ample preparation for a career? Yes and No. College has provided you with a body of knowledge and skills that will prove invaluable as you move up the career ladder:

- Your degree gives you accreditation which, by society's standards separates you from the non-degreed workforce.

- Your investment in higher learning developed skills which may be applied in various job settings.

However, all sources indicate that the average graduate experiences a great deal of frustration before finding a fulfilling and effective means of applying his or her learning. For some, this frustration may amount to a failure to find a job at all. Once a job is landed, a fresh onslaught of post-graduate shocks add insult to injury as stress and frustration mount to a frenzied peak.

The average graduate experiences a great deal of frustration before finding a fulfilling and effective means of applying his or her learning.

Academics provide you with theories and facts. Your advisors and instructors instilled you with information distinct to a specific field of study. However, they could tell you only so much about the application of that knowledge and still continue to speak to the needs of every individual in the class. Accordingly, you may manage to graduate and still not be able to come up with a highly specific answer to the recurring question, *"So, what are you planning to do with that degree?"* I know I annoyed many an inquiring mind by answering, *"What ever they'll pay me to do with it!"*

VALUE BY DEGREES

What immediate good will the diploma or degree provide? It will likely get you some graduation money and the praise of friends and relatives. It will probably provide you with a sense of accomplishment and self pride. With any luck, it will open some closed doors. But, don't be fooled, it holds no special powers after those doors are opened.

Attitudes—and realities—vary concerning the worth of a degree in the market place. New grads tend to think the BMW and Nakamacia home stereo system will no longer be restricted to the pages of a magazine, that living quarters will surpass that small cell shared with deadbeat roommates. Numerous hours of study and stress will, they suppose, be rewarded by an ability to accelerate in the 9-5 culture. Shouldn't society accept new graduates with open arms? Isn't it today's graduates who will bring new ideas and innovative concepts to insure culture's continued prosperity? Whether, as a college graduate, you invent a cure for AIDS or just a new coat hanger, you will contribute to the betterment of society —right? And a grateful society will reward you—right? Unless you are one of a few gifted and fortunate college grads, don't hold your breath. A diploma might place you on the correct road towards success, but it never guarantees it.

THE "9-5 SHOCK"

"Until the real world kicks you in the stomach and wakes you up, you don't understand that college is a different lifestyle," commented a recent Cedarville College grad. All new graduates will likely have their own definitions for the 9-5 shock, but five common traits are usually included in each student's so-called shock:

- confusion concerning their role in this new environment.

- a feeling of being unprepared due to incorrect or incomplete guidance.

- dissatisfaction with their financial status due to unrealistic expectations.

- dissatisfaction with their status and responsibilities in the work place.

- down-right fatigue and disenchantment.

Many of the recent graduates I interviewed gave some very specific answers concerning their definition of the 9-5 shock. The following entries paraphrase some very typical responses:

- a *social adjustment* inside and outside the work place (your social behavior is judged more severely once you leave campus and student status behind).

- a *culture shock* from the college nest to the cut-throat corporate culture (it may not be paranoia if you believe everyone is out to get you).

- a *financial adjustment* that may include a lack of money for even inexpensive leisure activities (see how much of a paycheck is left after rent, utilities, and the car note).

- the *realization* that you face the equivalent of 40 years of writing workshops or math tutoring (no longer are semesters measured in weeks, but rather years).

- *feeling like a freshman* without summer vacations (June, July, and August are no longer the sanctuaries they once were).

The 9-5 shock begins with realizing that the corporate world may not welcome you with open arms and a potpourri of fringe benefits. It continues once the job is landed and you are confronted with a fresh onslaught of shattered illusions and personal frustrations. They may have wined and dined you to get your services, but after day #1, the sweet talk reverts to a *"you're lucky to be here"* attitude.

The 9-5 Shock can be like a cancer, spreading untreated until it is too late. For the naive and eager, disillusionment can be particularly devastating. A college senior entering the working world is similar to the high school student entering the university. In both cases, many quit or transfer very early because of disillusionment, bewilderment, or an inability to see past their immediate discomfort.

Chuck Sunburg, UCLA's career placement director, observes

> *"Far too many students and graduates start way too late to prepare . . . they don't ever understand the job process. Colleges don't have the most practical curriculum for this purpose and they are not going to change."*

Many grads prepared four to ten years in the college ranks to enter the 9-5 world. Some did not even devote five minutes to prepare for the transition that can destroy the unwitting and the unwilling. As one 1987 grad explained,

> *"The transition adjustment is the last thing on your mind during your senior year, but as soon as you're out, you wonder why college didn't prepare you better."*

Another grad conceded that he was doing fairly well in his profession, but still adjusting to the workplace—8 years after graduation. Even after the big adjustment more or less works itself out, the working life continues to supply you with new aggravations.

John, a graduate of a small liberal arts school, crudely described his experience in coping this way: *"I never imagined it to be so stressful. All the surprises can blow your mind."* Although John found an excellent job a year after graduating, he said, *"Those first six months after graduation were hell."*

PROVING YOURSELF

So are you saying that my four years were wasted? By no means. Your degree puts you ahead of the game. Your advancement potential surely exceeds that of the lesser educated. Nevertheless, your diploma may not pay off (in terms of money or status) as quickly as you expected it to.

Several recent graduates concur that the degree has an immediate classification value. One Vanderbilt University grad, who owns his own consulting company, says,

> *"The degree automatically places you (favorably) in the 'with' rather than 'without' category. There is a class distinction between graduates and non graduates."*

Likewise, among students who are not attending school or are only credit hours short of graduation (for one reason or another), there seems to be a consensus that the *"piece of paper"* would greatly change their 9-5 status. As with so many other things in life, we appreciate an item more when we don't have it.

For increasing your ability to accelerate in the 9-5 world, the worth of a college degree can't be overestimated. Years ago, a high school diploma was the primary necessity in preparing an individual for entering the workforce. But as the market place becomes increasingly diversified and specialized, educational preparation also becomes increasingly specialized—requiring added years of education. Similarly, some experts suggest that degree requirements have become essential to insure a competent workforce due to the diminishing quality of secondary education.

It is also important to note that the degree serves as a tool for *"weeding out."* Employers usually associate a degree with *"stick-to-it-ness."* Whatever the value of a college degree, any graduate can't assume that the diploma is the all encompassing answer. The degree cannot stand alone. By achieving a degree, the 9-5 society allows you to take on other tasks that it might not allow non-degreed individuals to attempt. Graduating is an admirable accomplishment, but it is not the end. It raises you to another testing ground—the workplace, where you must prove yourself all over.

ASSIGNING RESPONSIBILITY

Who's to blame for the 9-5 shock? Identifying an ultimate cause is impossible. Many recent graduates blame their own naivete concerning what to expect in the working world. Some mentioned that the academic culture was a far too unique microcosm to be a good indicator of the future. Hear the words of two recent grads:

> *"It (college) was life under the bubble . . . college was not a correct forecast of what was to come."*

> *"College was so ideal: it shares wealth with all, always provides a welcome audience, has a supportive alumni. A graduate leaves this environment to the real world . . . it's a hell of alot different!"*

Apparently, these perspectives are rather common. Recent graduates suddenly perceive college as *"so ideal,"* or as *"life under the bubble."* Other words I heard were *"nurturing,"* *"comfortable,"* and *"accommodating."* Probably, these graduates would not have used these descriptions before graduation. But by contrast, the college world suddenly becomes paradise lost.

Remember that college also demanded adjustments from you. Also, no one paid you to go to college. You are working for a living now and you had better not expect the endeavor to be all bliss.

Maybe the college academic system doesn't require a complete overhaul. In all fairness, the system does seem to work advantageously for its graduates in the long haul. Employers obviously appreciate the value of a degree or they wouldn't insist on bachelors and even masters degrees for many positions. Then again, the same want ads which express preference for college graduates will usually make the additional requirement—*"must have experience"*—frequently requesting at least two years.

It is difficult to attribute blame in this situation. Are colleges failing students or are employers not investing enough in their own training programs?

The conventional approach to higher education found in colleges and universities has hundreds of years of tradition behind it. Certainly, higher education has responded progressively through the years to changes in society and the work force, but the classroom method of instruction remains relatively unchanged. The traditional method of college instruction allows colleges to provide its graduates with intensive yet flexible training. If employers are serious about their commitment to college graduates, perhaps they should take more responsibility for providing fresh graduates with the training required to shape effective employees out of recent grads.

Some colleges have made more effort than others towards complementing traditional classroom instruction with programs aimed at easing the transition from college to career. A thorough orientation process, similar to the freshman college orientation, could greatly reduce some costly and possibly avoidable problems for graduating seniors. Oregon State University, to name one example, offers *"Life After College"* seminars. Many recent graduates favor such programs and believe they are worthwhile. Drew University's president affirms the necessity of such programs by acknowledging that in *"most ways college is not a fair representation"* of the 9-5 society.

THE 9-5 SHOCK GRADUATE

Several types of graduates are likely to experience the 9-5 shock:

- Graduates who find that there job search continues way past their comfort zone.

- Students who find a job quickly but who find themselves performing tasks that are understimulating or which they consider beneath them.

- Students who basically like their work but who have trouble adjusting to the restrictive rules of the work place.

- Those who are unsatisfied with considerations such as money.

- Those who are experiencing confusion concerning their *"field of play"* or some other aspect of the 9-5 culture.

In other words, just about anyone can fall prey to the feelings of dissatisfaction associated with the 9-5 shock. In fact, most recent graduates attest to experiencing the shock to some degree.

For some, of course, the shock may stem in part from lack of academic effort. But even prowess with the books will be fruitless without a way to put the learning to use.

Take Brian, for example, and his adjustment into the corporate work place. Brian's college record consisted of a 3.3 overall GPA, several Dean's List citations, participation in intramural sports, serving as dorm director and student body senator, and memberships including the National Dean's List, school honor society, and fraternity. Brian also had many excellent letters of reference from past employers and professors.

Brian's 9-5 shock began with the realization that the job he had prepared so long for didn't seem to exist for him. Brian accepted the only offer he got, but resigned shortly afterwards due to *"feelings of uselessness."* Brian experienced six career changes in the following two years. In Brian's opinion those two years' frustrations could have been avoided if he had gotten better advice.

Similarly, Scott longed for graduation day. Little did he know that the next year would be *"one of the worst"* in his life. Scott had also achieved an admirable college record which included several Dean's List awards, all-star awards for varsity baseball, and membership in several college clubs. Although Scott was not a corporate recruiter's dream student, his credentials do not seem to justify two years of unemployment. Almost two full years after graduation, Scott finally obtained, in his words, *"a credible job"* with one of the country's largest builders. There were no great changes in Scott's work or education record. He was as well prepared immediately following graduation as he was two years out. Scott is still mystified when he ponders why this transition required two years.

Robin graduated with an English degree. She was very disappointed in her first job. *"Very little"* of her four years' education was utilized by her first employer. She quit one job after another. Thousands of dollars and numerous hours of a college education seemed to have led her to making copies and answering the phone. Robin is not alone in this dilemma.

Another graduate interviewed admitted that her decision to pursue an Master of Business Administration degree came mostly in the interest of escaping her 9-5 blues:

> *"At the time of graduation, I would have laughed at anyone's suggestion that I would willingly return to school in less than a year. I neither wanted or needed an MBA for any of the right reasons. But, I definitely did not like what I was experiencing."*

Many new graduates respond to their initial difficulty in adjusting to work by retreating back to campus. Of course, not every graduate student is a 9-5 deserter. For many, post graduate degrees will be highly appropriate. MBA's from good schools are becoming increasingly valued degrees. Post graduate degrees in other fields may also improve your marketability. Nevertheless, the 9-5 shock will be waiting for you when you return. It will take at least three more years and a third degree if you want to make a profitable career on campus.

These new 9-5ers felt betrayed and misled, having prepared so long for a job which either failed to materialize or proved to be immensely disappointing. For graduates such as these, insult seems to be added to misery when other students immediately succeed despite their apparent lack of qualifications. Brian, Scott, and Robin failed for no clear reason. Others students succeed for no clear reason. John, for example, graduated by the skin of his teeth. He received an offer to be an executive assistant at a large manufacturing company. John's college career consisted of playing varsity football and more varsity football. He minored in varsity football as well. But that is not to suggest John's only field of interest was one made of astroturf—his extracurricular activities included a passionate interest in beer and marijuana. It is still a mystery how John managed to graduate much less land a terrific job. Until the final exam, he did not know whether his cap and gown rental fee would turn out to be a waste of money. He used the outfit anyway and managed to walk off the stage and straight into a job which included an excellent salary, a company car, and an expense account. John landed this job by sending out a total of two resumes.

Whatever separates John from the millions of graduates who unsuccessfully struggle with incredible effort to attain their first job, it often is not what is commonly regarded as worthy credentials. Regularly, graduates whose qualifications are among the worst get a better job offer than some of the best graduates in the country. These outcomes upset many college officials, but little can be or has been done about it.

AVOIDING THE 9-5 SHOCK

The 9-5 shock will probably never be completely avoided. Most people are not going to take much pleasure from the realizations which a first job throws on you. Most first jobs aren't all fun and many graduates may experience the shock primarily because they are used to having more fun than they are allowed at work. I don't mean to sound trite or patronizing by suggesting this, but this component is at least a part of the 9-5 shock for many graduates.

Still, most people long for the ideal situation in which they can find work that is challenging, personally satisfying and rewarding. Hopefully, you appreciate the inherent rewards to hard work and perseverance. Still, most graduates don't realize that few people find rewarding and stimulating work immediately out of college.

If programs were implemented to address the college-to-work transition problems, perhaps we wouldn't see data like that generated by a recent Arizona State University study that found a surprising 40 to 50 percent of new graduates quit their first job in their first year. A great number of students interviewed were completely ignorant of this statistic. If first year grads were to know about such trends, a failed job effort might not seem so devastating.

A surprising 40 to 50 percent of new graduates quit their first job in their first year.

The University of Notre Dame's campus minister recently wrote, "*The trouble with many colleges is that they indulge the nesting instinct by building protected little communities inside their great walls.*" But until colleges stop nesting and many more begin following the example of Oregon State, students will not receive a realistic picture of *"the real world."* Dr. Patrick Sheetz, Michigan State University's Career Development Director, predicts,

> "*many more schools and professors are going to have to head in this direction whether they like it or not . . . . No longer is education solely for studying the stars. Academics need to give more realistic classes.*"

9-5 SHOCK SYMPTOMS

For many graduates the trouble of adjusting doesn't start until you become settled into a position. It might be a little like a hangover. Your brain is suffering throughout the night as you sleep, but it doesn't hurt until you awake. Unless its your nature to generally accept whatever other people wish upon you, the early symptoms of the 9-5 shock won't be hard to diagnose. Ask yourself these questions:

- Does your job become increasingly mundane (can you operate the copy machine with your eyes closed)?

- Is the morning wake-up call increasingly a time of dread?

- Have you often thought of calling in sick *"just this once"* rather than face another day at the office?

- Do grief and stress-management seminars at the public library seem like compelling topics?

- Does your patience wear thin at glib claims about this first job being a *"great experience"*?

- Do the morning classifieds become as desirable as the sports section or the comics?

As already asserted, the treacherous job search is only the first of a long-line of post graduate jolts. Even for those who quickly find what they initially perceive to be a promising and exciting opportunity, the adjustment has only just begun.

OVERCOMING THE 9-5 SHOCK

Unlike the first semester of college, the 9-5 shock has no precise, definite end. One group of grads said their personal adjustments lasted more than six months. The most common estimates indicated that most students will take 6 to 12 months to adjust to the work life after graduation.

Whatever the length of the frustrations that you may experience, remember that this is not a new or uncommon trauma. Many other recent grads are experiencing the same dilemma. Don't permit this temporary ordeal to sidetrack your future success. Stay alert to the quality of your work. Is your employer just paying a body now rather than a productive employee? Has your concern for excellence fallen steadily since that wave of uncertainty hit? Losing concern about a job is unfair to an employer and to you. Don't let a poor attitude cause problems now. A sour demeanor can isolate you from good references and from colleagues who might just hold the contacts to the job you really want.

Chapter Two

UNDERSTANDING THE 9-5 WORLD

You have recently graduated or you are approaching graduation. Your ability to immediately recognize the relevance of the following paragraphs will depend upon where you now stand on the college to career continuum. If you are just approaching graduation, resist the temptation to disregard the forecasts and warnings within these pages.

What can I expect to encounter?

If you are a recent graduate, the content of this book may ring all too true. Stop, if you have started second guessing every aspect of your college career in hindsight—from the quality of the diploma paper to your philosophy teacher's theories on the existence of God. Don't bother. It's now time to evaluate your talents and aptitudes and determine how they might best be applied towards advancing your personal goals in the job market.

Try to replace your sense of dread with an enthusiastic anticipation—look forward to analyzing the different players in this league, identifying the rules of play, and ridding yourself of old collegiate verities. Understand now that some of the old rules will not apply to your new environment.

This chapter gives a few examples of the types of difficulties that typically confront the recent graduate—difficulties most college students are unprepared for. Read carefully and ask yourself if you are prepared for all of the situations and dilemmas described. The chapter should provide insight which will aid you in devising a personal plan of action for alleviating your post graduate shocks.

So what's the first step in adjusting to the 9-5 environment?

Management experts recommend taking care of little things before attempting bigger challenges. This chapter's goal is just that. The first step in making the adjustment to the work place lies in being fully aware of your circumstances. Perhaps the very first step towards adjusting to life after college is realizing that if you are unhappy, confused and frustrated, you are anything but alone. Know that the 9-5 shock occurs primarily because of forces outside yourself; but, refuse to accept that the means to adjusting are outside of your control.

Understand why the shock occurs. Human nature allows us to bear up better under pressure when we understand its source. Furthermore, when you understand the source of a problem, you are better equipped to address it. College tends to send out graduates ready to conquer the world. The graduates are led to believe that they will find rewarding work if they do the right things. Furthermore, they are led to believe that they will find it immediately. A rude awakening awaits the graduate when he finds that the *"real world"* is not so ready to embrace him/her.

If you are experiencing difficulty adjusting to life after college, the most important thing to do is to keep your eyes on the light at the end of the tunnel. Know your goals and persist in pursuing them. If you are feeling discouraged now, it is probably because you were led to believe that graduation *was* the light at the end of the tunnel. Accept that you still have dues to pay and more to learn.

Keep your eyes on the light at the end of the tunnel. Know your goals and persist in pursuing them.

Why is college so different from the working world?

The rules of survival in college and the rules of survival in the workplace are somewhat different. You will find that many rules still apply but others will suddenly prove obsolete for no clear reason. College fosters certain traits which may contradict what an employer will expect from you as a rookie in the workplace. Once you have firmly established yourself in the 9-5 world, you may be able to shift back to the old rules to some degree.

For example, college promotes self-reliance and creativity. For your first year or so on the job, you may be discouraged to find that your employer expects you to subordinate these traits to conformity and obedience. Self-reliance may appear self-serving. Creativity may be equated with *"bucking the system."* Watch and wait before suggesting any *"improvements"* in any of your new employer's operations. You may have the best of intentions when you enlighten your co-workers in the error of their ways, you probably recognize a much better way of doing things; but, you must remember there are reasons why things are being done the way they are. These *"reasons"* may not justify doing things the *"wrong"* way. The *"reasons"* may even be unethical. Still, it may be too soon for you to be questioning anything. You will probably be stepping on someone's toes if you suggest there is a better way. Imagine the skepticism you might feel towards a rookie who waltzed into your veteran turf full of new ideas and suggestions.

College promotes self-reliance and creativity ... your employer expects you to subordinate these traits to conformity and obedience.

It has long been recognized that institutions of higher learning and institutions organized for profit operate under different principles and incentives. The most obvious distinction between the two is the fact that, while *you* pay for your education, once you become an employee, *they* pay for your services and will most assuredly expect a generous return on their investment. The exchange of money and the expected returns is the central difference between the two types of institutions. All other differences are derived from the money issue. For example, the grade is essentially the only incentive and monitor for your performance in school—you are paying for an education so that is what they give you. Accordingly, the criterion for deciding your academic standing is relatively objective and predominantly limited to academic performance—you either make the grade by successful completion of the assignments or you don't. Once on the job, you may find yourself judged on what will initially appear to be subjective standards—you feel you are completing assignments, doing as your are told, maybe a little more. But, someone may still manage to find fault with your performance.

Furthermore, the bosses' interference in your activities may infringe upon areas you once considered strictly your own business (e.g., how you choose to wear your hair, the clothes you wear, after hours activities). Why? Because the boss honestly believes that these issues have direct bearing on your success as a profitable company investment. Almost every 9-5 frustration common to recent graduates is directly or indirectly related to the graduate's insufficient preparation for the pressures of the profit-driven work place.

Once on the job, you may find yourself judged on what will initially appear to be subjective standards.

What are some of the differences I can expect to experience?

Every recent grad will have one pet issue that epitomizes for him or her the cruel adjustment from college to career. Still, in my interviews with graduates, there were some recurring themes:

1. **Complaints concerning the tedium of the job duties.**

    As a college grad, you are presumably hired to work with your brain instead of your body. However, every desk, lab, and/or field job requires many menial support tasks—especially in an entry level position. Be ready for the less than glamorous assignments. As you gain seniority and respect, your rights to delegate tasks down the totem pole will increase. In the meantime, you are a member of that lower region of the totem pole.

2. **Fatigue.**

   Working 40 plus hours a week will drain you mentally and physically. You may wonder how you ever managed to accomplish everything you did in college and avoid the mental fatigue you may experience as a new 9-5er who probably works from at least 8-6. The stress of the adjustment will aggravate your physical sense of fatigue. Be ready to make adjustments in your sleeping habits.

3. **Feelings of inadequacy.**

   Many recent graduates feel stymied in their ability to function productively in the first 60 days of a job. Employers understand that you will have to learn the ropes before you begin to really pay off; you may, however, feel like a bumbling fool in the mean time.

4. **Rude awakenings associated with office politics.**

   Jealousy and competition were probably only peripheral issues in your college career. Remember how much more begrudgingly the top-scoring student was treated in a class graded on a curve? Well, in a very real sense, you and your co-workers will be assessed against a curve as you compete for recognition and advancement. This situation fuels many of the negative aspects associated with office politics.

5. **Technical difficulties.**

   Copy machines, fax machines, computers, even the coffee maker may complicate your initial entrance into the working world.

6. **Learning to humble oneself to authority.**

   Even if you had part time jobs during college, you may have considered these jobs so replaceable that you rarely fretted terribly over a minor skirmish with your boss. Now, with much more at stake, you may find yourself so anxious to attain the favor of your boss that you begin humbling yourself to uncharacteristic lengths and then experiencing conflict with your pride.

7. **Receiving fresh lessons on the capacity for irrational, petty, and/or difficult behavior in human beings.**

   As a college graduate, you are probably not so naive as to think all people can be reasoned with or dealt with. But, your first real job may represent the first time you have to learn to deal with such people on a long term basis. You will have little to no autonomy in choosing whom you prefer to work with.

8. **Experiencing previously unparalleled pressures to perform with accuracy and efficiency.**

   Perhaps some of the hardest questions you had to answer during college were along the lines of *"Why didn't you show up for our date last Friday night?"* or *"Why are you repeating this class for the third time?"* The 9-5 world imposes questions which demand quick, logical answers. Why? The consequences are so severe. As Dan Akroyd reflects in *Ghost Busters*, in the real world, they expect results. When you are two days behind deadline, your boss is not likely to resemble the nurturing, supportive professor who gently reminded you that you were two months late in presenting him with a proposal for solving world hunger.

Business owner Gary Chelec explains what new graduates fail to understand:

> *"The more money involved, the swifter and more severe the punishment. At college, you could make up a class at 9:00 if you missed the 8:00 one. Work is one class, five days a week, Monday through Friday, with no excused absences."*

At least there will be no more studying, right?

Many college students anxiously anticipate the day when their duties will be restricted to only a 40-50 hour work week. Maybe you believe that no matter how miserable you find your working environment, at least you can leave it behind in the evenings and on the weekends. If you really believe this myth, share a few leisure hours with some people who really hate their work. It won't take long to discern that the misery arising from problems at work permeates every facet of their life.

Furthermore, the very phrase "9-5 shock" is something of a misnomer. You will be granted a very rare treat if your work day is restricted to 9-5 o'clock. For most, 8-6 is much more likely; for others, 7:30-6 or more is the reality.

Why does the work place demand so much of an employee's time?

The 9-5 employer considers you an expensive investment and intends to get as much out of you as possible. In many offices, you will find an unspoken taboo against leaving earlier than 6:30 or 7:00 at night. Perhaps no one tells you so in so many words but, if you skip out at 5 or 5:30 you may raise more than a few eyebrows.

Likewise, absences interrupt the work flow. Ask any employer if random unplanned absences are met with anything vaguely resembling approval. Time off is a must, but the work environment is not of the same make-up as the academic world. School operated with or without you; work might not have that same capacity.

While still in school, start enjoying the time off even more than before. You may want to take some time-off before you start work. Perhaps taking something of a retreat will be necessary to determine what you plan to do with the rest of your life. If this is not possible (and for most, it isn't), take an extended weekend vacation. Take a trip you've always wanted to take. Visit your grandparents. Starting work puts you at the mercy of the company. Enjoy free time while you can.

How do recent graduates describe work?

"I'm a machine", "I'm caged", "I'm a mule", "a monkey can do what I do", "I'm an object", "I'm a robot . . . there's nothing to talk about" is how Studs Terkel reports individuals describing their work in his bestselling book **Working**. For many white and blue collar workers, the job-satisfaction meter reads utter displeasure and despair. Is it all this way? By no means, but don't be disillusioned if your thoughts start to parallel such attitudes.

It is common to become confused or disenchanted with a first job.

If you're a rookie with ambition, you have to abide by your organization's decisions. Known in sports as *"riding the bench,"* at work, it's known as *"policing the xerox machine."* What? You mean they don't shove you in an office and beg you to take care of the Western Europe account? Not usually. Work can be painstaking drudgery. But if you understand that you have to work with a team and that you must walk before you can run, you will absorb the 9-5 shock more easily. Being the new player, you have the potential to bring new ideas and attitudes. How fast? Only you can determine how long it will take to break the *"freshman"* classification. Remember, you are new to the 9-5 world.

For recent graduates having spent their college career as full-time students, summer work has been the only exposure to the work environment. It is common to become confused or disenchanted with a first job. Adapting to the work world is an education in itself, it takes time to master the curriculum.

What are the rules of team play?

Another aspect of 9-5 life which you may not be prepared for is the concept of team play. Many will have no problem with this even though the past 4-5 years in college has been characterized by an every-man-for-himself mentality. Others may have problems with this concept even if they have an inability to see it as a problem.

The 9-5 environment means accepting responsibility for others, while others must accept the consequences for your actions.

The 9-5 environment means accepting responsibility for others, while others must accept the consequences for your actions. Josh, a computer sales rep from West Virginia University, explains this concept which many new 9-5ers have not been exposed to in the college setting:

> "A couple of other salesmen and I have to produce or our company will fail. Sure, my production is rewarded with commissions, but there are a lot of others who are

depending upon me to do my job. It gets to me sometimes. School demands were on me and me alone. A 9-5 job isn't that way, unfortunately."

In college, you were the only person responsible for your success or failure. At work, entire departments or divisions receive credit or blame for the fruits of your effort. The 9-5 society needs teamwork to avoid collapse and disorder. Veterans will have little sympathy for rookies that mess up the routine too badly or threaten their personal job security. Consider the major corporation whose rookie technicians created a chemically harmful material that was used in all of their new products. Years later this *"minor"* detail costs hundred of workers their pension plan investment for several years.

Susan, an '85 education major, explains her 9-5 shock in this manner:

"Learning to work with others is difficult. You're not alone, and can't pretend to be. This was the first time that I was ever in a position where serious consequences would affect a co-worker if I really messed up. It's scary, but you can't overly worry about it. Do your best, that's all they can ask you to do."

Paul, an '84 grad from Roanoke, Virginia, observes how he had to transcend his own narrow concerns in a new work environment:

"the initial departure from concerning myself with only my desires was tough. There was no choice. I had to get a job, make money, and get along with others I might not regularly choose. It was a tough adjustment."

Until now, your actions may have only been subject to approval by your parents and yourself. The reward and penalty system was also very different than what one may experience in the 9-5 culture. For instance, 9-5 paychecks and the approval or disapproval of your professors are slightly different incentives. If you got on the wrong side of a particular professor, you would simply avoid him where possible. Now, if you fail to please your boss, the implications are far more severe. How likely are you to get promoted? If you choose to leave is he likely to give you a praiseworthy recommendation? You are playing in a much different league.

How demanding will a normal job be?

Even if you worked before or during college, the post-graduate job is quite different. For one thing, you don't return to school in January or August. There are no month long *"recovery periods."* Many summer jobs could tolerate you showing up hungover, late, or ill-tempered. Normal jobs won't. One recent graduate I spoke to commented,

> *"Because I entered graduate school when most of my friends were taking their first jobs, I didn't understand why they all began to suddenly drop out of the weekday social scenes. I just didn't believe that work could be that demanding until I experienced it myself."*

He's not alone.

What can I expect in my first year out of school?

Going into nursing? Expect to see some bedpans. Ask any Cooper and Lybrand's new hire if their first assignment was glorified? Check with a bank's new manager trainee and see if they didn't spend some time shuffling papers? Obtaining a biology degree still won't prevent you from serving as a lab *"go-fer"* for a minimal time. Even an advanced political science degree which lands you in a White House intern position can't eliminate all the preliminary tasks (such as delivery boy) which most new 9-5ers will most likely confront.

If you have been led to believe that, *"Majoring in something will get you a job in that area of study . . . and then you'll call all the shots,"* as Elise, a 1982 graduate of Lehigh University was, then this chapter is a must.

This first year treatment is comparable to being invited to a frat party your freshman year. Confident that you are being recruited to pledge, you discover instead the fraternity's intentions include assigning you to pump the keg all night while some hot-shot member lures your girlfriend away.

As Dave, a 1975 grad, observes, *"Be ready for the real stuff. Many new grads have no conception of what the 9-5 is."* New grads are not equal to veteran workers in experience or knowledge. Bite your tongue and be ready in case you are treated as a freshman. If you're lucky, the boss will keep your talents and preferences in the back of his mind.

Greg, an 1982 grad, recalls when his company invited all the *"fast trackers"* to an elegant night of entertaining important customers. In anticipation, he vowed to become an expert on financial records to make a good impression. His superior intellect was finely tuned in preparation for any shareholder questions. However, he only spent the night incessantly murmuring *"Watch yourself"* as he opened and shut all the limousine doors.

Another frustration new 9-5ers complain of is conflicting instructions from superiors which fosters an inability to discern exactly where their *"field of play"* lies. A young computer programmer I talked to had been given several conflicting reports from upper management on the status of one job and the actions he was supposed to take in completing the job. He tried to diplomatically point out this problem to his direct boss. The boss assured him that the real confusion was coming from inadequacies among the *"lower level employees."* Bill says that it was all he could do to keep from shaking his employer by the shoulders while screaming, *"No, it's you, it's YOU!!"* In college, you answer to each individual professor as he requires. But, as the new kid in the 9-5 world, your obligations may not be so clear. You may be the one who catches the blame for confusion that arises from poorly defined chains of command. Or worse, you may find yourself playing the uncomfortable role of pawn in someone else's power play.

The first years out of school may bring a distinct feeling of insignificance. Teresa, a University of Alabama counselor, says legitimate reasons explain why work differs from initial expectations:

> *"College grads are inexperienced and have no past work record. They can't fit in day #1 following graduation. Employers don't even know if their new hire can act professionally."*

Rebecca, a 1982 University of Florida grad now working as a financial consultant, suggests that

> *"Organizing yourself is the first assignment. The 9-5 ordeal demands organization from you and all others. If you miss a deadline at work, it could well mean the pink slip. College conditioned you to work by yourself and for yourself. Entering the responsibility-oriented work world is a severe 9-5 shock . . . Employers have to start new grads off slowly until they prove themselves."*

College teaches you a thought process, but then a boss re-educates you to his methodology.

Don't be conned into believing that you're completely ready for work. College teaches you a thought process, but then a boss re-educates you to his methodology. Bosses have no choice—you are now their responsibility.

Rose, a 1985 grad working as a retail buyer for the May company, admits the changes are drastic:

> *"There is no longer any self pacing. How many hours are your own depends on when and what your employer wants done. Also, be ready to work around your co-work-*

ers' schedules. Since a new grad is low man on the totem pole, your time will be considered less valuable than anyone else's. There may be times when you are given an allowance for error. Other times, bosses will fire you without hesitation no matter how little chance you've had to prove yourself."

The learning pace of the 9-5 world can be frustrating, but as Gerald Kennedy, a Senior V.P. of First American Bank, explained,

"College grads have much to learn about working. It will not be learned in the first years . . . they have to be willing to accept that fact."

The raw skills are usually present for graduates just leaving the college nest, but it takes time to fine tune these skills. At the initial exposure to the working world, there are too many things competing for your attention. You will continually learn new methods for dealing with your particular situation. You will continue to mature. Each individual will blossom on a different schedule. Just make sure you continue to progress, accelerating at your own rate.

Chapter Three

PLOTTING YOUR COURSE

Since a job search can be an agonizing process, don't multiply your agony with a haphazard quest. Would you dare take your car in for repair without doing your best to guide the mechanic to the source of the problem? Allowing him to search cluelessly would run up a hefty bill in a hurry. Only you know what your objective is in bringing the car for service in the first place. When you provide a focused frame of reference, the mechanic can give you what you came for—nothing more and nothing less. Likewise, your career will be the most time-consuming facet of your life, don't allow your career path to be dictated by a *"hit or miss"* strategy. If you miss, you could be paying for it for a long time.

This chapter provides guidelines for setting your career priorities and keeping your short-term career goals in line with your long-term priorities. As a recent graduate, you will be faced with many options which will influence the development of your career. The following pages will guide you through some considerations which you might otherwise overlook and discusses some of the implications associated with the decisions confronting you as a recent graduate.

Do I have to know exactly what I want to do?

Of course not, but you should first concentrate on what you want to do before pondering where or when to do it. As you approach graduation, you should already have a fairly focused idea of the type of work you want to be involved with. After all, the past 3 to 4 years of your education has been spent in increasingly concentrated study. In other words, if you have just received a degree in accounting, this probably isn't the time to decide that you will have missed your calling if you do not pursue a career in nuclear physics. For most new graduates, a really radical change in direction is simply not feasible.

Concentrate on what you want to do before pondering where or when to do it.

On the other hand, there is a multitude of variables to consider in any field. You will be confronted with various decisions such as choosing an area of specialization, determining the type of corporate climate you want to work in, and deciding the salary you are willing to work for. The 9-5 shock can be considerably softened if your career path is properly matched with your personality and life-time objectives. This chapter discusses some considerations you should not ignore.

Is there a correct time to start looking for a job?

When do you start looking for a job? The end of your junior year, beginning of your senior year, Christmas vacation, or after you return from your graduation trip to Europe are all correct answers. There's no right or wrong time. Taxes and death are your only 9-5 ultimatums.

Employers do have hiring time frames, but there will always be jobs available in your field somewhere. If you desire to work for a specific company, your career center can assist you in pinpointing their hiring deadlines. As one recruiter explained, *"Not following our time frame doesn't mean you can't be hired, but, otherwise, the hill is much steeper to climb."*

First understand that a job means you no longer fully control your own time. You don't get extended vacations throughout the year. Vacation time initially consists of two weeks or less. If you hated college, you had at least a third of a year to recuperate and compensate. If you hate work, you only have about 1/25 of the free time to recoup. Kevin, an '87 graduate, half-heartily jokes, *"the thought of not having my summers by the pool is revolting."*

What if I choose to wait before seeking a permanent, career oriented position?

You may have some very clear, personal incentives for delaying your pursuit of a career-advancing position. Do what you feel you must do; but remember, fair or not, most employers are skeptical of graduates who *"waste time"* about getting a *"real job"* after graduation.

On the other hand, most employers will want evidence that unsettled restlessness is either settled or controlled. Rob, an '88 Wharton MBA, explains

> *"When you can sincerely enter a position with concrete career goals, you adapt naturally to the job. You need a couple of years after graduation before you can do this."*

Employees with ants in their pants are more of a risk than a recent graduate who is married, settled in one area, and starting a family. It's great to be able to tell a prospective employer that you have wandered around to your heart's desire, and you really want to settle down. Openly admitting this to an employer should be received as a real plus. If they convey any negativism towards your venture, be terribly careful before accepting a position.

Most employers will want evidence that unsettled restlessness is either settled or controlled.

Company executives read between the lines. They do look for reasons not to hire people. Appearing too unsettled is a common problem for new grads. Confront the problem head on. Refute anyone's worries by indicating that the *"unsettled times"* are over. Prove now is the time you choose to settle down and to adapt to the 9-5 culture.

Whatever your decision, the time void between graduation and the first day of work might present some problems. Two lines of thought deal with this free time. Both are very sensible. One view suggests taking an extended period of time off before starting work. Use it to travel the country or visit abroad. Use it to understand what phase of life you've just completed and what part you're entering. Considering the many years of a career, one or two years with a temporary or non-career type job may make little or no difference.

Nick, an 1984 graduate of UNC at Charlotte, who worked as a waiter for several years out of school, says,

> *"I get pestered all the time about not having a real job. But I want to travel, and to keep my peace of mind. Too many friends are completely stressed out by the time*

> they're 27. I'm enjoying myself knowing that I have a couple of years before I have to settle. People keep asking me if I'm sure, but I don't really care, because only I know my real self."

One fact Nick failed to mention was that he made more money as a waiter than many of his 9-5 peers. Put yourself into a position that you'll like, and in which you'll be able to work effectively. The timetable should always be a secondary consideration.

The second mode of thought places the graduate into the workforce immediately after graduation. For some, financial matters (school loans) make this the only alternative. Choosing to go right to work could eliminate any second-guessing and possibly give you a head start on other graduates.

Work, unlike school, does not permit *"bagging"* a day to go shopping, sleeping in, or going to the beach. Bosses can't do it. So why should you? Some people respect their time off so much that they risk their job. One young woman commented,

> "I've always wanted to visit Europe, and I knew I had to do it in the next couple of years. I asked for a leave of absence, which they refused, so I quit and went to Europe. You can't see Europe in just a few weeks. The funny thing is, I must have proved myself, because when I came back, they offered me my old job back."

One 9-5 Shock that employers hate to admit is the swallowing of pride when a good employee wishes to return, even if they improperly left. *"Getting, keeping, and replacing good help is not easy."* This is a common complaint amongst employers. If the loophole for returning is there, why not take advantage of it?

So how does that first job relate to my over-all career objectives?

For most, realizing that you still have dues to pay before *"arriving"* is about 90 percent of the post-graduate shock. In confronting your initial job search, think in terms of plotting a course rather than in terms of immediate arrival. If that first job is less than ideal, it will, at least, be bearable if you know exactly what you have to gain in terms of long-term goals. If nothing else, 6 months in any full-time position gives the illusions of *"real world experience."*

How restrictive should I be in determining the type of work I want to do?

As you begin your search, allow yourself latitude in determining the criterion which will guide your choices. Even though people will generally regard you with dismay if you can not come up with a highly specific answer to the question, *"So, what do you want to do with that degree,"* the truth is that anyone who thinks he knows exactly what he will be doing is usually fooling himself. Most recent graduates will not know precisely the career they want to pursue, many more will not have considered all of the alternative specializations, still fewer will have definite answers concerning such particulars as the size of the company they want to work for. Ironically, it is common for students who are most confident they know exactly what they want to eventually make the most radical changes in direction. Don't feel as though you must lock yourself into a decision.

To avoid hasty decisions and eventual disillusion, keep an open mind as you venture into the job market. Many individuals will find their concept of *"the perfect job"* will continue to evolve throughout the job search. The interviewing process itself often brings many previously unweighed factors to light. Keep your ears open, ask many questions, and read between the lines because the interviewer will likely be telling you much more than he or she realizes.

Should you find yourself second-guessing your initial objectives, allow yourself the flexibility to admit you may be moving in the wrong direction. Remain open-minded, but continue to zero in on the mix that will best suit you. By sharpening your focus you can avoid wrong decisions and maintain a sense of control. Before a productive career search can start, the seeker must have some inkling of the kind of occupation he or she can expect to find fulfillment in. For example,

> "I want something that will deal with computer maintenance and will allow me to earn between $18,000 to $20,000 a year, with at least two weeks of vacation."

That's an answer. Don't be guilty of overkill by limiting your possibilities, and don't feel as though you can't change answers.

How far can I venture from my original plan?

So, you have spent several years and thousands of dollars acquiring a degree which was presumably chosen towards some specific end. In a work force which is increasingly specialized, educational curriculum is likewise designed with a high degree of specificity. You probably were pressured into choosing a major somewhere around your sophomore year. But even if you were one of those rare freshmen who came into the college scene with your career and your life clearly and firmly plotted—absolutely certain of where you planned to be five years down the road—even you may be experiencing doubts as the time for graduation draws near. Maybe you have heard discouraging reports from those who have gone before you and now you're informing a dismayed and impatient father, *"But Dad, I don't WANT to be an accountant."*

Immediately prior to graduation, a friend of mine only half-jokingly commented that she had pursued a degree in business primarily because that's where all the good-looking guys were—and this from a magna cum laude graduate who was never your typical Mrs. degree candidate. Still, she was going through what many students nearing graduation go through—the realization that your degree will determine the type of work you are qualified to do and the fear that there is some other field out there which would be much better suited for you.

> *You will always have options. Continue to look for opportunities in keeping with your interests and skills.*

If you are feeling these types of doubts, first, slow down. Thoroughly analyze your feelings and consider all of your options. For many, this fear is primarily the product of a discouraging job search or an unrewarding first job. Are you looking for a scapegoat for your unhappiness or are your doubts valid? Look towards people who are several years ahead of you in your field. Do you consider their situation any more desirable, is it worth working for? How else could you apply your expertise towards a more rewarding career? Do you have the resources necessary to further diversify your training in order to broaden your marketability? Only you have the power to discern whether your doubts constitute a temporary set-back or the seeds for life-long feelings of regret. Try not to over-dramatize your situation, it is not unique and it is probably temporary. Furthermore, many people eventually find employment in areas more or less unrelated to their formal academic training. You will always have options; it is never too late to alter your direction. Continue to look for opportunities in keeping with your interests and skills.

What factors will determine my job search priorities?

Determining your destiny overnight is impossible. First, consider strengths, weaknesses, and interests. Look back at what you enjoyed doing most in college. Did you like working with lab partners, or did you prefer to work by yourself? Did you like doing oral presentations or turning in papers. Do you only request a hefty weekly paycheck, or do you demand job challenge? Perhaps you want the imaginary job where you're paid for sitting in an office all day with nothing to do except read, catch up on your correspondence, and drink coffee.

Understand yourself before trying to sell your capabilities to an employer. An informal job search strategy can help a great deal. Before fully developing your strategy, you can begin focusing your objectives by answering the questions below:

1. **Areas of Expertise:** What is your educational background? Did you select your major or did it just happen? Can you find rewarding work in this field?

2. **Personal Involvement:** Do you like being involved? Does the job permit a comfortable degree of involvement? Do you prefer to do things yourself or work in a group.? Will you perform behind a desk or out in the field?

3. **Commitment:** Do you need to be dedicated to a cause? Do you look out for yourself? Are you capable of humility? Are you willing to make sacrifices? What do you consider a long week? What comes first—family, recreation, personal fulfillment, monetary gain, etc.?

4. **Working Conditions:** Is the company socially similar to the college you attended? Are you used to know-

ing people? Do you prefer personal attention or are you self-taught?

5. **Superiors:** Which professors did you like and why? Are you capable of dealing with people you don't like? Can you subordinate your self to an individual you don't particularly like or respect? (Be careful of prejudging superiors. First impressions are often incorrect. If you look back over the experiences you had with instructors during your academic career, you will probably think of instances which validate this point.)

Your answers to these questions should provide some guidance. If you are tempted to dismiss these guidelines as useless career-counseling propaganda, don't. Believe me, I felt all that career search information was nothing more than garbage. Although I am now a vice president who enjoys several fringe benefits—getting here was not easy. I am certain the struggle could have been alleviated with some good advice. If only one or two bits of information prove extremely useful, your time was well spent. *Graduating To the 9-5 World* aims at providing some tools for easing the transition from college to the working world, but *How You Really Get Hired* and *Careering and Re-Careering For the 1990s* are excellent sources in helping a new grad find their career direction. No book will give you all the answers, but they can provide some starting points.

How important are starting salaries?

Don't get hung up on figures when it comes to starting salaries. For what seemingly is a great salary now might prove to be peanuts three or four years down the road. In other words, don't have your head turned by an impressive starting salary which may not grow with you.

Don't choose between the two absolutes of liking your work, but not your pay, or getting a lot of money, but hating what you do. Try to do a little of each. Don't let early career satisfaction depend on how much money you make.

As with nearly every issue touched upon in this book, there are as many answers to the money question as there are different types of personalities. We all know people who will suffer any degree of boredom or misery if the price is right. On the other hand, there will always be those people who scorn monetary gain and thrive on a sense of personal satisfaction which they find irreplaceable. If no amount of money can compensate you for being bored out of your skull, be wise enough to shun the lucrative, but tedious, job.

Unfortunately, money can often seem to be the only factor because of hefty school loans. As one grad joked, *"I received all this schooling for what? I guess undergrad and medical school was to put you in debt over your head."* Ed, a recent graduate now working as a District Attorney for the city of Houston also admits financial difficulty, *"School loans are a must, but they are an enormous load to absorb following graduation."*

Don't focus on a starting salary when considering a job. Instead examine the salary potential in the short and long run. The factor of money, in your first years out of school, can be very deceptive. Many 9-5ers flabbergast employers by refusing job offers because of a measly $500, when in a few years their actual salary will be much greater. When you agree to a starting salary, insist on periodic reviews accompanied with possible pay increases. Be aware of the purpose your job will serve for you. Is it experience or is it money that you need most at this time?

Remember to look down the road a bit. A college graduate is an attractive commodity, but a college graduate with a couple years work experience is far more valuable. You are just starting this career game, not finishing it.

How should I consider benefits in relation to salary?

All the time and energy you invested in gaining your diploma may automatically program you to calculate upcoming paychecks in terms of hard, cold cash. As so many other things in this 9-5 shock ordeal, the compensation issue is not as simple as it seems. So many of you will see compensation as *"starting salary range,"* and fail to understand that the compensation package is so much more. It's sort like a nice restaurant advertising a premium meal at one price, that main item really gets your attention but the side dish prices is what *"shocks"* you. The *"side items"* of any compensation package is what can be surprisingly good or bad.

At the time you reach a salary negotiation—and not before—don't look too naive by exploring in great detail the insurance deductible on the first interview. Divide the issue into several distinct topics. Just as important as the issue is *how* you approach them. As stated earlier, you are a rookie and being too cocky can allow your negotations to result in, *"we'll call you if we need you."* Tread lightly, and politely, but do tread on these subjects. Otherwise you might not receive what they were willing to give. Remember companies are on budgets.

Understand that each situation is unique. Several factors influence the final outcome:

1. **Whom are you talking to?** What authority do they have to offer what benefits. A vice president will certainly have more power to offer more benefits than a campus recruiter.

2. **What is the size and status of the company you are dealing with?** Is that industry overwhelmed with grads seeking any type of position at any type of pay just to get some actual experience, a foot in the door? All you have to do is compare the journalism field to nursing in this era to see that supply and demand certainly applies to the job market.

3. **What position are you in?** Can you walk away knowing there are three other offers sitting at home or is this the only offer that has been extended after 4 months of concentrated effort?

Plotting Your Course 45

Take these factors into consideration before you sit at the bargaining table. Assuming you are fortunate enough to reach this status, consider the following aspects along with the starting salary. A combination of many can easily outweigh one large aspect.

- **Salary:** Look at the salary and how it is structured. Are you paid salary, or hourly? Making $750 a week for 40 hours could be much better than an $880 salary which requires a 75-80 hour week. If overtime is involved how is it calculated (1.5 or 2 times regular wages). When are reviews and under what criteria do they work? Find out what a typical salary will be in year two or year three (there is probably no need to look past year three unless you have access to a crystal ball).

- **Taxes:** How will your salary be affected by taxes where the job site is? Would it be better to stay in one area making less money with no state or local taxes. Or would the taxes be insignificant in comparison to the increased wages a job in a high tax area offers. Case in point is, my first move to Texas was a pleasant surprise when I noticed a larger take-home pay due to no state taxes versus my home state of Virginia. Don't only find out what you will gross in pay, but what elements will decrease it. Remember when you are being recruited the pay terms are always in *"gross dollars and not in take-home."* There is a difference.

- **Insurance benefits:** Such benefits are great bait for any company to catch a prime college graduate with; but, below the surface that bait might be an expensive benefit. Ask many questions when it comes to the insurance issue.

    - How large is the deductible (what you have to pay), is there more than one deductible.

- Are prescription drugs covered, emergency room visits, dental, eye care?

- Are dependents covered under your policy?

- Is the plan effective from day one?

- How does the billing operate?

- What aspects does the plan not cover fully?

- Were any services discontinued from last year and have any been added?

The insurance issue can be very complicated for a new grad to grasp. Three simple suggestions—find a friend in the insurance game and get some insight to what a good typical plan consist of; compare each company to the others whom you interview with; and finally use your campus career guidance counselors to help you sort out what constitutes a good plan vs. a bad one.

- **Vacation time:** The amount of vacation for a new graduate is usually the standard two weeks. There are employers that grant more and some that grant less. You must determine how your vacation time may be taken. Are you allowed to be creative in your scheduling? Can you spread your vacation time out over the year or do you have to take it all at once? Ask the following:

  - Is vacation mandatory?

  - Is it paid vacation?

  - Do you get sick leave in addition to vacation time?

- Can vacation time be cumulative/carried over to the next year?

- Are there certain times of the year vacation is not allowed?

• **Profit sharing opportunities:** This area will vary greatly depending on the industry you are in. But examine what offerings are available to you:

- Are there any credit unions? A classic example is a job that offers $1,000 less, but has a credit union with much lower loan rates than you could get elsewhere. The credit union advantage might easily outweigh the lower salary.

- Are there any bonus rewards (trips, gifts)?

- Is there a stock purchase plan? Does the company contribute?

- How long must you be employed to take full advantage of the plan?

- Is there a savings plan such as a 401k?

- Is there any type of end-of-year bonus if the company exceeds its goals?

- What about a retirement plan? Social Security alone will not cut it.

Don't be mislead by a salary figure alone. Assume as little as possible to prevent any misunderstandings. And if you know of future events you want to attend, make requests for this time.

• **Company accessories:** Will your new employer provide for all your tools or will they be your responsibility coming out of *your* paycheck? An offer that includes a company car might be worth several thousand dollars on a yearly basis.

Look at what your job might require. Then, determine if the company will support these additional costs or will you be the bearer of these added expenses.

The list could continue on, but the situation and the environment will be the determining factors. Still, consider these factors that other grads mentioned they wished they had asked about before they accepted their jobs:

- Is the job subject to layoffs? What good is $65,000 a year when you only work 3 months out of the year?

- Is there an educational reimbursement plan? Who qualifies and when and for how much?

- Is there security provided? If the environment dictates security does the company provide it?

- Is there a signing bonus (rare but it is available to a few)?

Be smart, be diplomatic, but leave no "benefit" stone unturned.

Be smart, be diplomatic, but leave no *"benefit"* stone unturned. Not only is it in your future best interest, but, also, a smart interviewer will be impressed by your inquisitiveness. One employer commented, *"I assume a prospective employee who asks no questions has little respect for him or herself."*

What about the relocation question?

It really doesn't matter where a young college graduate begins a career. You probably know other graduates who moved away following graduation but moved back home within a year. Likewise, many graduates leave with the intention of coming home as soon as possible but end up deciding they can not leave their new home. This decision is highly personal and you should consider all of the implications of moving or staying.

Perhaps you refuse to even consider the possibility of leaving. Then again, you may have decided nothing less than getting as far away from home as possible will suit you. If you are torn between moving or staying, consider these issues:

- Does your hometown really offer promising entry-level positions in your field?

- Are you kidding yourself about being able to survive so far away from friends, family or lover?

- Can you withstand a slump in your social life?

- If you choose to relocate, will you enjoy experiencing a new lifestyle or will you long for the familiar?

- What are the cost of living differences between your home town and the one you are considering relocating in?

A strange surrounding will make you more independent and give many new perspectives. You can be challenged in ways you wouldn't be at home. For example, if you're asked by your boss to put advertising in the local papers, you will have to do more research and make more decisions than if you'd stayed home. Leaving familiar territory eliminates the use of crutches.

Remaining in the same location has as many advantages as well. It's easier to adjust to the 9-5 society if you stay in your home territory for a while. Knowing where to escape to, or whom to visit, and where interesting people hang-out are a valuable tool in battling the weekly 9-5 stress. If you're away, you might be challenged just getting home every night. Tom, originally from deep southern Virginia, says sarcastically that he wasn't having any problems adjusting to northern New Jersey, *"I have to concentrate so hard to just survive the morning and evening rush hours here,"* he confessed, *"that I don't have the energy left to think about how miserable I am."*

You may decide that you would like to be as adventuresome as Tim, a former law school student I interviewed. Tim always had thoughts about traveling Europe. One day he quit his job at the U.S. Patent Office to tour the European Tennis Circuit. After fulfilling his commitment to the tournament, Tim returned home to law school. The bug bit again. Shortly after his return home, Tim was invited to be the head tennis coach for the nation of Kuwait. In Tim's opinion, there will always be law schools, but he could not pass up the opportunity to coach a national tennis team.

Also consider seemingly insignificant areas that will affect your work picture. Veteran 9-5ers insist that recreation potential influences your happiness or displeasure with a job. If you move to a remote area with little social activity, what will your work attitude be like?

Whether you move or settle, advantages accrue either way. So stop worrying and get on with things.

Once I know what I want to do, how am I supposed to find it?

You may not find your niche right away. The important thing is to identify the course you want to take. Again, think in terms of long-term goals. Will this first job be a logical step towards my ultimate objectives? Why choose an immediately desirable but ultimately dead-end job? Appreciate the long-term advantages of a job which may require some personal stamina and endurance on the front-end but which will ultimately prove worth while.

> *The important thing is to identify the course you want to take.*

Furthermore, if you are caught in the *"highly educated/no experience"* catch-22, you may find it absolutely necessary to spend at least a year in a less-than-desirable position. Try to stay within your field, but don't worry terribly if the job holds very little resemblance to the work you eventually wish to pursue. A future employer will probably be most interested in the fact that you were able to hold down a job at all. One great fear employers have of recent graduates with no experience is that, in spite of their textbook expertise, they will prove to be incapable of applying knowledge and performing the mechanical duties of a given position.

You run less risk of selecting a job that makes you unhappy if you can choose from many options. Chapter Four provides some guidelines for organizing your job search. The general idea is to keep your priorities in mind while not ruling out any options.

Chapter Four

ORGANIZING YOUR JOB SEARCH STRATEGY

Although any number of things can factor into securing a job, resumes, contacts and interviews are the elemental components of a job search. *Resumes* provide prospective employers with a formal, impersonal presentation of your qualifications. *Contacts* allow you to learn of an opportunity—they can be as personal as your next door neighbor or as public as an entry in the classifieds. *Interviews* generally come last and provide a person to person assessment of what you have to offer an employer and vice versa. Chapter Five is devoted to the interviewing process; the other two components are discussed in the following paragraphs.

What purpose does a resume serve and just how important is it?

A resume is just one piece in the complicated employment puzzle. Without the other parts, a resume is only worth the value of the paper it's printed on. Resumes are essential, but they are only one tool for getting what you want.

The resume is the first opportunity for an employer to evaluate your skills. It is a document that allows others to determine if your qualifications match their needs. It seems as though students think of resumes as the magic answer to their problems. The information on a resume plays an important role in providing an opening for you. It may get you the interview, but it won't get you the job.

However, I do not mean to down play its importance. If the resume fails, you fail. For those companies that receive thousands of resumes a year, the resume will likely hold greater importance. In any case, the resume must accomplish two things at the beginning. First, it must catch someone's attention (the secretary or the personnel manager). Second, it needs to intrigue the potential employer. If your resume is successful, the hiring process continues; if not, it ends.

What makes an impressive resume?

Your materials must first be neat, timely, and impressive. Don't write your letters on napkins or legal paper. Make sure they're signed, stamped and mailed. Certainly, include your name, address, and telephone number. Laziness and carelessness impress no one. By all means, consult some resources in composing your resume. *High Impact Resumes and Letters* by Ronald L. Krannich and William J. Banis is an excellent resource on this subject.

How much exaggeration can I get away with?

It is generally understood that people will use more lofty language in a resume than they will in casual conversation. Describing yourself as having *"excellent oral and written communications skills"* is certainly more appropriate for a resume than saying that you *"talk and write good"* (or even well for that matter). On the other hand, if you claim to have *"played a key role in the development and implementation of an advanced interactive computer-based training program"* when all you actually did was plug in the machines, expect to be put on the spot and embarrassed if you even make it to the interview stage.

For many people confronted with the task of compiling a resume, it is difficult to discern between the laughable and the impressive. You may want to seek consultation or feedback from more experienced parties if you fear you can not make this distinction. For anyone entering the job market for the first time, it is probably a good idea to get as much constructive criticism as you can find before you begin submitting your resume.

Make sure your resume stands out, but be careful. When I was constructing my first resume, I went to my father's office to look at resumes on file so that I could compare styles and approaches. I was also interested in getting some feedback from various people in the office concerning what resume techniques they found effective. One of the men in the office happened to be screening resumes for a position he was attempting to fill. He showed me one in which the applicant boasted *"photographic memory"* and *"no physical limitations"* as well as the ability to *"efficiently and flawlessly perform all work assignments."* The implication seemed to be that no task was too great for this applicant as long he was protected from some accidental exposure to kryptonite. His claims were not quantifiable qualities; he said little of any legitimate credentials. Furthermore, even if he were every bit as efficient as he claimed to be, nothing touched upon in his resume had direct bearing upon the job in question. Most employers realize anything that sounds too good to be true, probably is.

Don't pretend to have skills you don't possess. Certainly, don't say anything that can be refuted by one of your references or past employers, and don't say anything you can't back up in an interview.

Many college students' imagination can fill a resume. Riding an air-balloon once, for example, doesn't make a person an enthusiast. What happens if your interviewer or new boss is a real expert? Does paying dues to an association/club each year, without ever attending a single meeting make one *"an active four-year member."* While it is true that most resumes tend to lend a degree of false importance to their subject, if you go overboard you could find yourself in a very embarrassing situation.

> *Don't pretend to have skills you don't possess, and don't say anything you can't back up in an interview.*

When the resume states items such as GPA or major, the accuracy had better be perfect. For any variance with these, or other items that are easily verified or refuted, can cause an interested party to terminate any further interest. Assume that employers will investigate the accuracy of these claims.

Aren't all resumes essentially the same?

Imagine the millions of letters that the college recruiter for IBM gets every year saying the same thing: *"I need a job!"* IBM doesn't have enough jobs for all the talented, worthy graduates who want to work there. You weren't the only one on the honor roll, the varsity basketball team, debate team, or having a double major. Many others also have great references and previous work experience. The numbers game is against you. Someone will always have a better work history or a more attractive resume.

By all means, alter resume styles and presentations to fit the variables for different companies. You risk failing if you decide to be aggressive or vary significantly from the norm. Who cares? You will pursue enough possibilities to endure a few losses along the way.

Try different attacks. For example, you are bound to make an impression by returning your original rejection letter when you reapply to a company. Your cover letter this time may include an explanation why they should hire you now. If you have already been rejected once, you have little to lose on a second time around. Prove you have ambition, persistence, and a real desire to work for them. Rabbit's feet and four-leaf-clovers will not help. You have to slant the odds in your favor. We are all individuals, yet we pursue our goals in much the same way.

Most of us seek our jobs in exactly the same manner as everyone else: get the name of a company, send them one cover letter and one resume, and wait for a response. A warm search, directed at individuals, is much more effective than a cold search. Sending out *"Dear Sir"* letters by the ton usually results in a ton of disappointment. Is a send/wait job search method sufficient, or is *"a gang buster"* attitude required to get a good job? Only you set your own destiny? For some professions and industries the send/wait is the only way.

Make sure your approach is suitable for the job. Don't use the same for a bank as you would to an advertising firm. Consider corporate personality and the traits they likely prefer in employees. Will they be impressed by creativity and imagination or are their employees models of conservatism and yuppie conformity.

You may want to experiment with some of the following attention getters:

- cover letters with **charts, famous quotes,** or **different printing styles.**

- a **floppy-disk presentation**—you'll get a response or the disk won't ever get past the magnet.

- **videotape**—expensive, but attention-getting.

- **unusual contacts** with executives, such as mailing a resume to their country club or home address. Catch them off guard.

Experiment to your heart's desire, but expect the worst and hope for the best! You will experience some wasted efforts. But you may also receive a response from a company who will send you a ticket and ask you to fly out for an interview! Bowater Paper liked one of my proposals. I didn't get the job, but I was able to enjoy two beautiful days in South Carolina when they flew me in for an interview.

Should I turn my resume over to a professional resume writing service?

There is no cut-and-dry answer to this question. Be very careful about whom you trust to do your resume. In the first place, they may not be qualified. Furthermore, so many people rely on these types of services that the work of a professional resume writing service may be very recognizable to an employer who sees a lot of resumes. While the mere fact that an employer recognizes that your resume has been professionally done may not be a problem in itself, it is a problem if the language of the resume echoes that of many other resumes passing through the office. Furthermore, your resume can not possibly stand out if it is on the same stock of stationery as 50 others as well as being in the same style, font, and format. In other words, you do not want your resume to appear mass-produced. If you go the route of a professional resume writing service, go to special lengths to ensure that your resume does not bear a strong resemblance to a hundred others circulating throughout your community or the country.

But what if I really need help writing and designing my resume?

Unfortunately, many people graduate from college without the writing skills necessary to compose a presentable resume. If you are uncomfortable with your writing skills, you are not alone. There are many alternatives to the professional resume service. If you're lucky, you may have a friend whose skills you trust. If not, you may consider contacting the head of a writing program at a local college or university who could recommend a student writer or editor. Students generally work cheaply and they are likely to have access to desktop publishing or word processing facilities. If you have any doubts as to their qualifications, check into having an instructor oversee the student's work. This is only one alternative but, if you are resourceful, you should be able to track down someone who can assist you in preparing your resume for circulation.

The resume is the first opportunity for an employer to evaluate your skills. It is a document that allows others to determine if your qualifications match their needs. It seems as though students sometimes mistake resumes as the lone determinant in being hired. It plays an important role in providing others insight to your work habits, but it is only one tool for a successful job search.

Should I network?

You may be fortunate enough to find a job by responding to an ad in the newspaper. Certainly, this is an established and viable way of learning about an opening and attempting to attract the attention of the person hiring. Likewise, sending our resumes to personnel departments for companies who hire in your field may net some responses. But if you are serious about your job search, you will have to complement this approach with some more aggressive measures.

As you begin your job search, you may be very frustrated to find peers who possess questionable or unexceptional qualifications landing desirable jobs while you fail to get any offers at all. If this is the case, it is probably time for you to learn how to gain and maintain good contacts.

We have all heard the statement, *"It's not **what you know**, it's **who you know**."* Usually this statement is uttered with a great deal of cynicism. You may be one of those people who feels as if the words *"networking"* and *"connections"* should be catalogued under *"unethical practices."* We can all agree that it is unethical when a lesser qualified person receives a job simply because the employer was afraid of loosing the applicant's father's business. And it is true that many less than admirable deals may be made in the name of networking.

Still, there is no reason why you should refrain from using interpersonal skills and contacts in implementing your job search. If a person hires you because she knows you, it is simply because the things she knows about you are good things. The employer prefers to hire an applicant about which he/she has some personal knowledge.

The employer prefers to hire an applicant about which he/she has some personal knowledge.

There are few employers who have much to gain by hiring someone *"as a favor."* At the rate of thousands of dollars a year, granting employment is an expensive favor. You will not be hired unless an employer thinks you are worth the investment, so don't refrain from pulling any strings available to you. Put yourself in the employer's place. You have two resumes in front of you. Each candidate looks very good on paper. One applicant, you have some personal knowledge of. The other is a complete unknown—even if this applicant appears (on paper) to have slightly better qualifications, you may prefer to hire the individual whom you have a personal knowledge of. Likewise, you'd probably prefer an applicant recommended by a respected associate over a competing applicant whose references are also unknown to you. While credentials will always be important, you can not tell much about a person's character or his/her interpersonal skills from a resume.

The truth is no one can succeed for long on the wings of their connections. On the other hand, no matter what your credentials, your career prospects can be exceedingly improved by making yourself known to many people.

Accordingly, you should not use and manipulate other people. The idea here is simply to learn how to make yourself noticed by the people in a position to hire or help you. Make sure that you are more than a piece of paper or a set of credentials.

What holds more importance for the new graduate, who or what you know?

Allow me to answer with another question, *"which came first the chicken or the egg?"* In all my research, the answer seemed to be split right down the middle. It seems as though the academic profession professed a stronger belief in what, whereas many recent grads and 9-5 executives favored who (for some, the advantage of utilizing contacts never wears out, but for others it does).

This great variance in answering the question "who or what" can be accounted for rather easily—within different professional communities, the influence of whom you know will vary respectively. But, while the perceived importance of contacts varies, most everyone had some knowledge of a case in which the *"who you know"* appeared to be a determining factor in success.

There is little dispute to the importance of *"what you know."* Students, faculty, new grads, and employers all agree the more the better. Fortunately, there is not the circle of politics to contend with in improving *"what you know."* Common sense dictates that *"what you know"* should greatly exceed the importance of *"who you know,"* but, the 9-5 game rulebook doesn't always make sense. Play it safe, put forth all your efforts in making contacts, and then impress others *"with what you know."* Eventually, those contacts are going to want to test your knowledge.

I remember a fellow banking trainee, the son of a prestigious financier, who had every possible connection at his fingertips. My colleague refused to use or even divulge his contacts' names. His quiet, unobtrusive style made his progress assured. For some, just knowing they have an inside track gives an indefinable air of assurance, confidence and success.

A rookie 9-5er can benefit tremendously from the help of others to get a good career start. One executive interviewer commented, "Who you know is much of the game, not only for a new graduate but for anyone in the game of life." Carlisle, an '84 graduate expresses her opinion, "the standard line that contacts are everything is sad but often true."

New 9-5ers must receive training, guidance, and counseling from others. The more acquaintances you have, the more potential friends and helpers. Learn to develop reliable contacts; don't aim only for quantity. "Getting names is easy, but correctly using them is the difficult part," comments Jim, a recent graduate from Wake Forest University.

Proven contacts can bridge the corporate communication gap. They usually give sincere advice. They can help all along the way from selecting your first job to choosing when to retire. From getting an interview to surviving office politics, contacts, used correctly, can only help.

"If I'm aware of a person because of a personal contact," commented one personnel officer, "I might ignore the mistakes they make at the beginning of the interview and just see if they've made progress by the end. Otherwise I might quickly end it."

Contacts are crucial in today's market, stacked as it is in favor of the employers. "All I have to do is place an ad or call a local college, and instantly my desk is flooded with resumes," comments one Washington, DC employer. A recent grad working on Capitol Hill said, "If my boss mentions the need of some administrative help, the office gets swamped with some very impressive candidates."

Contacts can often lead to the best interviews. In my own senior-year job search, 22 of 36 interviews were the direct result of such a contact. It need not be your long-lost best friend. It may just be the friend of a friend.

Many businesspeople consider their contacts absolutely essential to their ongoing career survival. Many further note the importance of maintaining contacts outside your profession, your age group and your community. New graduates, especially, may be in need of developing interpersonal skills which transcend demographic boundaries. In college, you were probably settled in to a very homogenous group of friends. Perhaps you neither wanted or needed to consort with people whom you did not already share much in common. If this is the case, you need to make some very deliberate efforts to learn to interact with people you might not otherwise choose to know. As Jimmy Koons, president of the world's largest Ford car dealership, said, "*Graduates are used to dealing with their own. In the working world you have to learn to deal with all types and, more importantly, all age groups.*"

Excellent qualifications guarantee nothing. Many over-qualified graduates cannot find satisfactory, interesting work. On the other hand, several thousand graduates get wonderful jobs each year—some don't deserve them and never will. Take John from Chapter One. He might someday run his father-in-law's company. Unfair? Of course it is, but who ever said that the ability to perform simple addition and subtraction were prerequisites for running a company?

Jeff, an '85 finance grad attending law school at night, talks about his company:

> "It's amazing to see the number of grads that get in because of Daddy. Daddy doesn't even have to work here. He can work for a company that does a lot of business with the employer. Think about a top salesman who earns one or two hundred thousand from one client. Don't you think he'd get that client's child a job to save that commission? You're darn right he would!"

How does one attain and maintain good contacts?

Compare your potential contacts to a garden. The most fruitful plants might stand hidden away from the openly exposed plants. They may not make the most attractive garden, but they produce more. Contacts are a dime a dozen, but good ones require notice and cultivation. That's your job. The more seedlings you plant, the more possibilities you create.

But you can't just plant a seed and expect the fruit to magically appear in your Jello salad one day. The dilemma of getting good contacts is similar to an employer finding good people. A boss may be happy to get two good applicants out of a hundred. Likewise, many college grads complain yearly about the lack of effective contacts. It's a two-way street.

> *Contacts are a dime a dozen, but good ones require notice and cultivation.*

How to I make contacts with strangers?

It's easier to ask a friend for a favor than a complete stranger. It's easier to refuse a stranger than a friend. This works in the job hunt, too. The more you know someone, or appear to know them, the more attention you receive.

The types of people who represent potential good contacts are also the types of people who appreciate friendliness— even friendliness from strangers. You probably know someone who has an uncanny ability to attract and befriend people. You may be mystified by her talent. But the ability to make people like you is really no mystery at all.

The following tips are not novel or unique. You may very well be tempted to yawn as you read through them. You will tell yourself that you know these things already and will proceed to skim briskly through each entry. Don't. So you've heard it all before—but have you really applied these interpersonal skills? Read the following entries carefully. Read them several times. Read them every morning if you have to. But decide now to make them a part of your business/social life.

Remember names and address people with their name frequently during a conversation:

- **Look people in the eye and smile.**

- **Listen—really listen.** Many people call themselves listeners, but their body language communicates that they are only waiting patiently for the other party to shut up so that they can say something truly worth hearing. Don't be guilty of this. Think about someone you consider a sincere listener. How do their posture and facial expressions convey their sincerity?

- **Keep your eyes and ears open** for subjects that will appeal to a potential friend. One subject that appeals to everyone is the subject of self. Find ways of discovering a person's interests. Everyone goes about throwing around the query, *"How are you doing?,"* yet few people exhibit any real interest in their fellow man's well being. Be a person who shows some real interest in others.

- **Go that extra mile.** *"Do unto others as you would have them do unto you."* If you're waiting tables, don't have a *"it's not in my job description"* attitude. You never know whom you are waiting on. Open doors for people. Smile and be friendly in elevators. Be a nice person.

- **Chat and indulge in small talk** at every opportunity.

Again, the foregoing is probably no revelation to you. I am sure that you already have ideas that could be added to this list. The point is, in the midst of a job search, it is particularly important to concentrate on making conscious applications of your people skills. The wise person will continue to make such conscious application throughout his/her life. Being a nice person has its own rewards. This chapter is not meant to encourage the *"what's in it for me?"*

attitude. But, I see no harm in pointing out the fact that making friends has rewards beyond your social life.

Do you expect me to just start approaching people on the street?

I don't suppose I would go that far. But, if you can make it work for you, go for it. Seriously though, it is true that potential contacts can be found right under your nose. While you can't count on acquiring a job from a person you meet at a cocktail party, it is not at all unheard of.

Can any acquaintance become a "contact"?

The most ignored category of contacts are individuals encountered on jobs held during or between college. Too many people discount the high potential of getting terrific leads from these jobs. A New Jersey bar owner told me, *"I remember very few college workers ever asking me for help. Little did they know that some of their customers were very influential people in the 9-5 job market."* He recalled a waiter who just graduated with his degree in computer science. The waiter had unwittingly served lunch every other day to the president of a local computer company. Such leads can be your first step, they are the easiest leads and the most overlooked.

Leads may be hiding where you work. Steven, an '84 graduate, said interviews at school and local company offices never produced anything, but discussions at his job (a health spa) were very productive. Why? Steven is in familiar surroundings, knows the people and the procedures, and can project a capable, positive image. If you get a chance to talk business on your turf, don't give it up. True, your contact is in the driver's seat, but you have the chance to select the car. One health spa lead landed Steven a job which is producing over $100,000 a year!

Some alternatives to immediate career employment are restaurants, health clubs, temporary services, construction, and resort areas. They are all excellent sources for developing contacts. Jobs with high customer contact have better chances of producing leads than jobs without. Scott, a current student at Rice University said, *"My job as a check-out clerk at the grocery store has netted me some great potential contacts which could very well prove useful in a job search."*

Wherever you make your network, remember not all sailing will be smooth. You may be rejected more often than helped. Some people won't give you the time of day. But don't waste time regretting them or trying to get even. People may later remember your hasty words and ruin your chances. Don't burn a bridge you might need to cross one day. Mr. Paul Edge, senior vice president at a firm employing more than 600 people, said,

> *"A bad meeting can ruin a great work record and eliminate a good possible connection. I just had a three-year manager refuse one final request that would have taken a half a day. I'll be damned if he ever works for me again."*

Contacts will be futile if they are not handled properly.

Surprisingly, rejections are also excellent sources for developing contacts. You will receive many rejection slips in a thorough job search. I know, I got 85. They hurt, but don't throw them away. Make a file so that you will have the correct name to contact when you're searching again. Stay organized. When you reapply, make sure your original contact is still there. Then send a copy of the first letter with your new resume.

A good rule of thumb is *"three strikes and you're out."* If a company or individual doesn't respond after three efforts on your part, write them off, and go get busy on that next attempt. Don't waste time worrying over it—you probably wouldn't want to work for them anyway.

Bob, an '88 graduate of Marymount University applied umpteen times to his local county police department without any luck. He finally decided to use other contacts. Recently, one of Bob's contacts opened a door enabling him to enter into a branch of his county's law enforcement.

Similarly, I applied to the U.S. Coast Guard five times between 1978 and 1985. I was finally accepted on September 10, 1986. I didn't spend all this time just applying to the Coast Guard. I had other jobs and goals along the way, but I never gave up. My determination eliminated one *"what if."*

Realize that employers are not always going to answer, interview, or hire you, no matter what contacts you possess. Keep going anyway. Some employers fail to respond to test your motivation. Yes, this is rude, but many feel that if you accept their first refusal without trying to change their minds, you must not want the job. One girl was so appalled at not getting the job after her interview that she called the company and informed them that they had made a mistake because she could do the job best. She told them to hire her. The firm granted her another interview and extended an offer shortly thereafter.

How do I turn an obscure acquaintance into a potential contact?

Determine one of his or her interests, learn some tidbit about it, and mention it at the next opportune time. A small conversation can easily lead to a future favor. Barry, who works at a large insurance company, knows one fellow employee who could have passed as Pee Wee Herman's long-lost cousin but who turned out to be a beneficial contact:

> *"One day I was in his area and noticed a Chicago White Sox headline pinned to his bulletin board. The next day, my comment on the box score sparked a lengthy discussion. I did not know or ever want to know anything about the White Sox. But the next several months passing each other in the halls included 'How 'bout them Sox?' And all those 'How 'bout them Sox?' did result in receiving an enormous favor from this gentleman."*

"The more you know, the more qualified you are" is a 9-5 law that often provides an outstanding chance to get a desired

job. But, the law of contacts is frequently stronger. It's only limitations come from a person's willingness to remain positive and persistent.

Be creative in acquiring names. One graduate I interviewed said he gains names at his health club from the name tags on gym bags. This is just one example, the possibilities are endless.

Be assertive in finding necessary information. Who would know about a job first, someone who reads the classified sections or someone who knows a department head? If you contact someone other than the personnel manager, you might get a little extra attention. It could make all the difference.

Do the extra work, return calls, send self-addressed stamped envelopes to their offices, or whatever helps you stand out. Writing a letter saying you are considering a career in Human Resources and would appreciate some time to discuss the profession could lead to an interview. But remember that being down-right deceptive will result in negative consequences.

In many cases, the chances of a contact paying off are slim; but, nothing ventured, nothing gained. Remember that every attempt can be chalked up to experience and either used again or abandoned.

Again, the rule of greater risks equaling greater returns holds true. One 1987 graduate tells of convincing the president of a computer consulting firm that he wanted to do his landscaping. The grad explained how it would be good publicity for his (mythical) new business, since the president was such a popular community leader. Actually, the grad was looking past this job towards the possibility of working in the consulting firm's accounting department. The landscaping job afforded the graduate the opportunity to strike up a friendship with his customer. The following winter this resourceful young man abandoned his landscaping job for an accounting position in his former customer's company.

Get the attention of prospective employers and prove to them that you are worthy of consideration. It's certainly easier to send one letter and hope and pray you're invited to an interview than to pester and demand one. And, of course, neither approach works every time. James, an '85 art design graduate, said his unique approach backfired at first, but netted him a job in the end:

> *"I wanted to show my aggressiveness and creativity, so I drew a pie diagram of my qualities and listed honesty as one of them. However, the percentage I listed for honesty ruined my equation, showing the rest of me was a crook. Fortunately, the employer understood my point. He really stuck it to me, but we both ended up laughing about it."*

James took a chance and won, but other bosses might have condemned his talents to the trash can. Counting on one contact to land a job restricts you to exactly that—one chance.

Only you can find the job that puts money in your wallet. It takes many tries and many promises. Promises are plentiful, but cheap. Depend on one person—yourself!

Whatever the purpose for developing the contact, put persistence into your formula for success. One refusal to answer your request is not the end of the world. And make specific requests.

One New Jersey company had a good idea that a new grad could use in making contacts. They sent all the classmates of Robert, a 1985 marketing major, a postcard informing everyone of his new real estate position. The $10 investment could result in several thousand of dollars for Rob's company. If any recipients ever move to New Jersey, they will likely call Rob first. You can probably think of ways of adapting this concept to serve your personal situation.

What if I have always been shy and will have to start at ground zero in acquiring contacts?

I would be lying if I said that didn't make a difference. I would, however, still dispute your claims of not being able to make contacts.

Most people spend four years studying in order to get their diploma. Just from going to classes, living in a dorm, participating in intramurals, and doing laundry periodically, develops contacts, that is—*acquaintances*. Those who have none feel cold, lonely, and confused—like Linus deprived of his blanket. Don't be a graduate who feels stagnate and stranded by lack of contacts.

Start to build your network in your freshman year of college. This is more a process of remembering names, faces, and interests, than a deliberate spider web. Be able to associate names, faces, and identifies when the need arises.

Use your campus career placement office

Job-seekers often use the college faculty, staff, and administration either too much or too little. If your college has a career placement office, start visiting it during your junior year to find out what you need to know and do. Then do it. One South Carolina school recently started guaranteeing that if a student follows its prescribed career guidance and graduates with a 2.5 or better, then he or she will have a job within six months of graduation. If not, the school will refund $2,000.

Career placement is often ignored, but many great leads and contacts can be generated from it. Make the placement office aware of you, and make it recognize your credentials. Don't expect miracles—you can't drop a resume off and sit back waiting to be called. That is lazy.

But, placement offices work hard to help the willing. They have a vested interest in helping you find a job—every career center's success story is a selling point to prospective students. Unfortunately, several large universities say their career centers are the most under-used tool on campus. Not getting an offer out of initial visits might cause dissatisfaction with the system. Placement is not assured, if it's not pursued.

Joy Flowers, a career placement director for the past 10 years, acknowledges the underutilization:

> *"Every year a great number of students ignore or incorrectly use the university's facilities. The best advice, which proves effective every year, is for students to start early and do deep research about their possible careers."*

You can sift through hundreds of business directories if you honestly want to, but why not bypass that and use sources that want to help? Yes, it's true—a good contact is worth a thousand pages. Books can give all the information in the world and not a single *"inside"* lead. Books give information, people do something with it. Use your career center's people.

Don't forget your professors

Although placement centers often offer the best college contacts, don't ignore professors. They do reward students who apply themselves by assisting in the job search. Consider the following guidelines before asking for a professor's assistance:

1. Are you on good terms?
2. Have you given him your best work?
3. Is the professor involved in student affairs?
4. Does he have practical experience in the workplace?
5. Is he popular?
6. Does she conduct seminars for companies or groups?
7. Is he involved in the community?

Use a professor network, but first prove that you can still do your homework. Be prepared with resumes, cover letters, and lists of potential employers. Do the legwork, then ask for advice. Ask more than one professor: a single choice could be wrong and ineffective.

Professors know many past students in a number of professions. Just remember that they have classes to teach, and can't babysit you through your search. And, again don't become solely dependent on one resource.

You might even try school or community guest speakers. They are difficult to reach, so exercise your ingenuity and display your determination. Pick them up from their hotel, send them a drink or wave a large sign that says "I NEED A JOB!" during their speech. *"I felt my chances to be recognized were small,"* recalls Scott, an '84 grad who did wave such a sign when a large conglomerate's chief executive spoke at his school. *"But, at least I had a chance."* Within reason, exhaust all your possibilities. Remember the more the risks, the greater the success or failure.

Become involved in professional and social organizations

Organization memberships prove useful if you treat them seriously and not just as another resume item. If you did pull your own weight, then the potential contacts are out there. But don't abuse the privilege or expect immediate results. Imagine what might happen if you found an interviewer was a member of your fraternity? And that you both served as fraternity treasurer? Need I say more? Leon, a sales representative for a major soft drink manufacturer recalls interviewing for a new position with a fellow alum who, like Leon, had been on the swim team. He was thrilled when the interviewer announced, *"I think I'll have a good chance of us getting along just fine. I can't imagine these similar traits doing anything but helping."*

Use alumni contacts

Without a question, alumni are fantastic contacts! This is particularly true of colleges and universities which are characterized by a particularly strong sense of school loyalty.

Begin attending alumni meetings. Alumni are usually very supportive of fellow and future graduates, no matter what year or class. Don't expect a job solely on the basis of your alma mater. But you can greatly expand your contacts through the alumni network. An extra effort will enable you to meet a lot of people, some of whom can directly help, and others who will provide valuable names to contact. Listen well at alumni meetings.

Go to the alumni office and ask for a directory. Find out which people are in your field. Don't write them letters asking for a job on the strength of sharing a college. That's idiotic. Instead, seek advice. Try a letter along the lines of

> *"I researched college records and discovered that you have done quite well in merchandising (or whatever the area), and I would greatly appreciate several minutes of your time."*

They might be willing to help you, and might even suggest something that bears fruit. The more successful the individual you contact, the less hesitancy he or she should have in helping you.

The first alumni meeting is always filled with intrigue. Everyone wants to know who is doing what. Smart people make sure everyone already knows what they're doing and refrain from dominating the evening's conversation with a blow-by-blow account of life since graduation. Instead they have called their friends regularly and kept in touch by Ma Bell. You'd be surprised how word gets around, especially within the alumni grapevine.

Networking is a game of reciprocity

A contact relationship doesn't cease when you land a job or are granted a favor. You have to nourish your contacts. Offer to help them in exchange for their help. You and your friends will separate as the years go by, but you should stay on good terms. You can't keep in touch with everyone, but old friends are invaluable aids. I have observed my father help family friends over the initial hump. In return, I have received numerous helping hands from his contacts. Don't expect immediate advice or assistance when you give. Request assistance graciously. If a friend's help comes through, so much the better. If not, you must still show your appreciation for their efforts. It's no different than work.

Sometimes you fail there, and companies continue to issue paychecks.

The benefits of maintaining these relationships can span an entire career—and outweigh measly considerations like phone bills and writer's cramp. Jerry Tolsen, president of Pride Office Supply, said, *"Letter writing is a great habit. Those little pieces of paper won't be forgotten like a phone call. Most of us should write rather than call."* There are more benefits than companionship, intimacy, and sympathy in a friendship. But to get the extra benefits, you have to exert yourself that extra mile. Letter writing is just one example.

People will not help you if you haven't contacted them in four or five years. Fair weather friends are really obnoxious. So are people who don't return a favor when they can. Don't overdo a good thing. If a contact isn't asked for a favor every time you call, he will be more inclined to help you when you do request it.

And if assistance is given, be certain to show your sincere appreciation. Don't just thank a contact verbally—give him something he'll appreciate. That's what he has done for you! A neighbor of mine wrote 10 different recommendation letters for my Coast Guard effort. You had better believe I wrote a thank-you letter! Flowers or some other token of your appreciation may be in line.

The extra effort might just make the difference between your resume and someone else's. Whatever the results, don't stop at these sources: keep making contacts everywhere.

Compare your caring of contacts to the operation of a car salesman. If he thinks your deal will lead to future references he will really try to get you exactly what you want. If he sees you as a one time shot, prepare to pay full price.

If you are fortunate enough to make a good contact, don't waste it. Don't let your contacts down. They stuck their neck out for you, make sure they don't get blamed for your performance.

A veteran 9-5er explained, *"I never mind helping young grads as long as they don't disappoint me. When a recommendation proves correct, it's a plus for me. However, if an individual fails, I fail, and I don't need any help in making mistakes."*

An '84 grad described how he committed such an error with a friend's father:

> "I was told that he would set me up if I was certain I would follow through. Three weeks after having been given a chance at his friend's company, I quit. I had placed a very valuable contact in an uncomfortable situation."

Are certain contacts better than others?

No contacts are bad contacts! Although a lead might prove to be useless, that same contact could someday be very worthwhile. Understand that contacts can remain dormant for a long period of time, and without notice become very important. If all contacts are good, a wide variety of them is even better. Don't overlook anyone as a potential contact.

Reap long-term rewards

Networks help throughout life, not just after college. For example, one interviewee's father knew the chief executive of a major airline. Her teenage brothers have missed their flights several times, and the only way they got on booked flights was because her father knew someone. You don't have to be particularly close to those people, but you do have to remain on good terms. Be prepared to do the same for others if they call on you.

Pretend you have three friends: one a car salesman, one a bartender, and the last an intern at a law firm. With luck, you can get a better deal, an extended happy hour, or some extra attention to your case. The possibilities are endless, but you must, must, must return the favor. Whether you're dealing with friends or business associates, all take and no give catches up with you very quickly.

Many people keep business and social life separated. This is not always easy, necessary or wise. If neither party asks for anything illegal or unethical (and what true friend would?) what harm is there? Don't expect friends to give services away, but it's not wrong to receive extras. Joan, a 1983 University of Texas graduate says,

> *"Because I'm a manager, I can treat friends and preferred clientele a little better than others. Some claim that this is unfair. I say it's good P.R."*

Finally, use contacts with patience and realism to gain expertise and added perspective in the 9-5 culture. Rather than trying to be the expert in all, know an expert in everything. Having all the latest book knowledge will not alone overcome all the problems a new 9-5er encounters. Accompany your knowledge with good contacts. Using them fosters success. Not using them may keep you from applying the knowledge you do have in the job you want.

The other side of the networking game

Jealousy and jeopardizing others' reputations are two risks associated with utilizing contacts. Jealousy may be petty, but there are measures you can take to see that you are not a victim of jealousy. Likewise, a reputation need not be marred by a contact relationship.

People may talk about how you got your job. As long as you are confident in the integrity of your actions, ignore them. Contacts may push your resume to the top or help schedule your interview, but from there, you're on your own. Don't feel guilty. You built your own resume, this contact just helped turn the light on it.

No matter how you use your contacts be prepared for others to gossip. One graduate who experienced the jealousy of co-workers, said of his first job experience, *"After six months on the floor I overheard the rumors. Not only was I the supposed president's spy from Harvard, but I was to be responsible for massive layoffs."*

The best way to deal with these types of attitudes is to not sink to the level of your detractors. Persevere and know that your talents and qualifications will prove true in the end.

Another pitfall in the contact game is the possibility of

communicating the idea that you consider your contacts more important than your abilities. Name-dropping is universally considered an unattractive practice. If you get an interview because of a contact, it might be smart to not even mention his or her name during the interview. Both rookies and veterans agree that contacts can be useful and impressive when not flaunted. If overdone, it's risky, even insulting. Credit assistant Lorretta Thompson, a veteran 9-5er, commented *"If a recent graduate starts throwing a lot of names at me, I automatically detect an ego problem."* Contacts can backfire, if you incorrectly apply them at the wrong time.

It's great to get a job entirely on your own talents. But you might get a better one by swallowing some pride. Positioning yourself favorably with a contact is playing smart ball. It may open a door that would otherwise stay shut. You speak for yourself at the final interview, but it never hurts to have a few doors opened on your way there.

Contacts will lead to open doors, and even have closed ones opened for you. Contacts might also preclude you from many tasks that others must complete. Unfortunately, they can even secure an unworthy promotion or raise. There is no doubt *"who"* can be a great advantage, but only you can gather all the *"what."*

Chapter Five

THE INTERVIEW

What is a job interview like?

Interviews vary greatly from situation to situation. The personality of the company and the interviewer will determine, to a great extent, the dynamics of each interview. But do not underestimate your influence upon the progression and outcome of an interview. If you're well prepared, there are many ways you can subtly take charge of the interviewing game. Of course, you should never appear to be the one leading the interview. You must remain deferential in demeanor, but, you may still manage to direct discussions in your favor.

The key is to be prepared. You have no way of knowing how each prospective employer will go about getting the information he wants from you. But you can go into an interview knowing what you want to communicate in the time given to you.

An interview can be a confrontation or an opportunity to exchange information with a prospective employer. This portion of the hiring process is, for most employers, the most valuable element in deciding whether or not to extend a job offer.

> *An interview can be a confrontation or an opportunity to exchange information with a prospective employer.*

What are employers looking for in an interview?

Interviewers are looking for evidence to support or refute the claims on one's resume. If you are unprepared, it will become evident after several interview questions. Employers know what they need answered, be ready to give them your thoughts. The 9-5 workplace spends millions of dollars each year on bettering their interview skills. It might be wise to counter with some practice of your own.

Employers are risking a great deal of time and money with each new hire. They want to ensure that their interviews are worthwhile predictors of one's work quality. Aside from your resume and a background check, employers have no other means to determine who you are. Interviews are frequently the final chance for interviewers to prove or disprove their *"gut feeling"* about an applicant. Interviewing is very serious business.

Of course, some interviewers will ask ridiculous questions like *"What role does country music play in your life?"* and never bother to check your excellent references. Others will try to put you in the hot seat, just to see how well you perform under pressure. You're at their mercy, but you can adjust the results if you're prepared.

What types of questions should I be prepared for?

The nature and number of questions you have to answer may amaze you. The company is trying to base a hiring decision worth thousands of dollars on a few hours of information. Have you ever tried to draw the correct conclusion about a girl or guy from their yearbook picture? That's what employers are doing until you come to an interview. Interviews provide insights that resumes and transcripts and references cannot. Today's printing technology can make an average person extraordinarily attractive on paper. Prove you are not just paper pretty.

Prove you are not just paper pretty.

An interviewer's imagination is the limit as far as the type and variety of questions which may be asked of you. The following are fairly typical. You should at least have anticipated answers for questions such as the following:

- **Collegiate Choices:** Why did you select your college, your major?

- **Personal Questions:** How do you spend your spare time? What are your interests? Do you like to travel?

- **Career Objectives:** Where do you see yourself in the next five years? What do you expect to accomplish in the next three years?

- **Work Environment Priorities:** Big or small company? High corporate image or laid back atmosphere? Do you perform well under deadlines? Can you handle constructive criticism? Do you work with a team? Will you work weekends? (What they want to know is if you'll fit in with their office climate.)

- **Personality Questions:** What is your greatest weakness/strength? Are you ambitious, organized?

And what are the correct answers to these questions?

Presumably, interviewers know what they are looking for when they ask such questions. Obviously, more goes into your desirability as an employee than your ability to match your skills with the job description. Still, for most interview questions there is not one right answer. However, some traits which would always be advisable to demonstrate would be dependability, competence, and integrity. For the interviewer, the general idea is to get you talking and to see exactly what you will reveal about yourself. Think about how you draw your impressions about the people you encounter socially, at work or school. Most of us know better than to put a great deal of credence in what a person explicitly says about himself/herself. Be very conscious of the messages *you* are placing between the lines.

The list of questions provided above is quite cursory. If you can remain undaunted and confident no matter what questions are cast your way, you will do well. Also, remember to answer questions in the context of the company where you are interviewing. If you can honestly tell them what they want to hear, do it.

How do interviewers assess applicants?

"An interview allows me to read between the lines," comments Darwin Seibert, a veteran of more than 500+ interviews and 25 years in the 9-5 workplace. *"After a couple of interviews, a*

person will start to provide some real hints to their work habits. It's not like resumes where they can dress-up phony claims."

When you're going to an interview, realize that the company starts with the advantage, but you can determine how much of an advantage they keep. You will be nervous, and you'll probably show it. You may begin to relax by admitting your anxiety to the interviewer on the front end. But, do what you can to get over it. The important thing is self-control. By all means, don't faint, throw up, or run out of the room in hysterics.

Peter Anspach, a business owner who hires many grads, revealed, *"No matter what company, what tests or special routine an interviewer uses, their decision is a gut reaction two-thirds of the time."*

Many employers will attempt to better understand who you *"really are."* Some may try to extract the *"truth"* by being very polite and soft spoken, while others might pursue intimidation tactics. The styles of interviews will vary greatly depending on the personality of the interviewers. Expect anything and you won't be caught off guard.

Approach each interviewer with a positive self image. Beat him to the punch by preparing your thoughts and doing a little research on the company. Pretend it's like finding out what's going to be on the test before you walk into the classroom.

Some professional books insist that you have to follow the same attitude and approach throughout all your interviews. That's fine if you keep interviewing at the same company, for the same job, with the same person. Be creative in your initial approach, continue to be creative and interesting at your interview.

In a certain sense, you can approach your interviewer as you would a stranger in a social situation. You can usually make some inferences about a person's personality on an initial meeting and, usually, you respond to them accordingly. For example, if you meet someone who appears to be very reserved, refined, and proper, you respond to them somewhat differently than you do to and exuberant, unpretentious sort. If you were intent on gaining either person's favor you would use different approaches for ingratiating yourself to their different personality types. The only difference in an interview is that your response should *always* be geared towards pleasing the interviewer. Be sensitive to the personality types you find around you in an interview situation. Do you want to work with these people? If so, what type of person do you think they will want to work with? You may not use this same tactic in all of your interactions with strangers, but then most strangers don't influence your career.

Don't let them think you've used up all your intelligence in getting the interview. Practice makes perfect. You may want to try out new approaches in interviews that don't hold great importance to you. Confused? Let's say you want to work as a stockbroker for Shearson/Lehman. Don't count solely on your role-playing abilities. Prepare. Line up interviews with smaller brokerage companies. Experiment with different approaches. You have little to loose and much to gain. And by all means, keep an open mind about *any* company you interview with.

Many experts suggest sure-shot answers for closed-door situations. They say such responses can enhance your ratings. Forget a format. Interviewers almost never ask you the questions you can answer easily. Be yourself—that is who they will end up getting—but be prepared.

What are the best answers in an interview?

The best answers are the honest ones.

What seems insignificant to you may be a gold mine to an employer—You're not a loudmouth; you just have great communication skills. You're not a loner; you can take responsibility upon yourself. You're not just a waiter; you've demonstrated that you can handle people well. Be creative, but not fictitious. Some employers do check references, and you won't be hired if you've lied.

If an interview gets a little bumpy, change to a new tune. A good example was an answer I borrowed for the question *"Jerry, you've told us about your strengths; now tell us of your weaknesses."* My answer was *"I've told you of my larger streng-*

ths, now let me tell you of my smaller strengths." Both interviewers stopped and commented that that was one of the best answers they had ever heard to that troublesome question.

Feel free to use that—I'd be flattered! Any answer's effectiveness depends on who hears it and how it is delivered. If an interviewer says he thinks an answer came straight out of the book, then politely throw the response right back at him. Tell him where you got the answer. Mention that you prepared by reading several books and attending sessions. Make sure your responses indicate your interest in the job!

Many employers are expecting a presentation—my interviews with employers confirmed this. Don't just regurgitate your resume, highlight details and traits that can't be effectively put on paper. The following are traits that many employers expressed as being very valuable in any employees' character.

- **Accuracy:** sell yours as a tool of profitability and predictability.

- **Honesty:** your integrity will help the firm keep its profits.

- **Flexibility:** show yourself willing to do anything reasonable at anytime.

- **Enthusiasm:** sell yourself as the new transfusion of energy.

- **Reliability:** sell yourself as free from bad habits, able to follow instructions.

These alone might not substitute for a strong GPA or test scores, but excellence in these areas can improve any record in the eyes of an interviewer. If you select to promote these qualities, be prepared to display actual events, even if it is the way you stack your woodpile. Don't make claims without the ability to tell how and why.

Emphasize the unique skills you don't usually discuss. A double-jointed wrestler has a subtle, but definite, edge over other wrestlers on the team who might be stronger and quicker. Unless he explains his hidden advantage, however, a coach might overlook him because of his evident weakness. If you can surprise a boss with the importance of a trait you possess which he has missed, he will remember you.

Mark, a computer/accountant sales rep explained how he interviewed with his present boss: *"I wasn't an expert in any aspect of accounting like some classmates, but told him I was willing to learn to be one."* In this case, his boss ignored his lack of expertise and acknowledged his desire to learn.

Other equally important qualities sometimes get overlooked. *"Maturity and savvy are intangibles, but ever so attractive,"* mentions one 9-5 player.

Ann, a Washington, DC interviewer, advises, *"Be a person willing to do anything with a smile."* Sounds like a small insignificant attribute, right? It is, but what happens if the interviewer is surrounded by negativism throughout the office. A continual smile might just be what the *"9-5 doctor"* ordered.

The value of any interview depends on both parties involvement. Do your share, be prepared with what you want to say. Before advertising yourself as an attractive commodity, know what and how you plan to present your qualifications (common or uncommon).

Are there questions that an employer is not legally allowed to ask?

Yes, there are a great number of topics that interviewers are not allowed to delve into. A good guideline is that any question must be directly related to the job. If an interviewer starts asking illegal questions, don't retaliate with the threat of a lawsuit. Beat a cheater at their own game. Dish out more information than they might ever expect.

For example, perhaps a question is directed at what your mother or father does. First, identify the question as being one that does not pertain directly to you. Second, respond wholeheartedly. Explain that your father has had the same job for 20 years, your sister has been teaching at the same school since graduating from college, and that your teenage brother has been pumping gas at the same gas station all throughout high school. Point out the attitude of company commitment in your family.

If companies want that information, give it. But wouldn't it be funny if your father had the same job but with 19 different employers, or that your sister only graduated three months ago? And maybe your teenage brother has a prison record. That answer has absolutely no bearing on you whatsoever, but it is truthful—if not the whole truth—and sounds good.

Give employers evidence that personal matters are a reflection of your work record. A good personal life, a stable credit history, and a variety of hobbies can make an employer see you in a favorable light.

Why does this illegal questioning go on? One, it does provide an employer with some valuable information that they might not otherwise gather. And two, most interviews are behind closed doors. Then, it is only your word versus theirs.

Can you effectively prepare for the many variables of an interview?

Try the following crash interview prep course. Mix personal experience, past interviews, and role playing with a friend or relative to ready yourself. Even if you think role playing feels silly, it can reveal something you might otherwise overlook. If this game reveals that you rarely look straight forward or that you constantly bite your nails during interviews, then the silliness was all worthwhile.

Obtaining information about a company will help you prepare for some interview questions. Talk to competitors or firms in the same field about the company. Research will give you new ideas to inquire about when approaching any company. If your research shows that the Better Business Bureau, several stockbrokers' business reviews, and college career center directors gave the company good marks, telling the interviewer this information might impress him with your interest.

Asking for a copy of the job description before the interview is a good plan. I wish I had done so before interviewing for a model planner position with a paper company in South Carolina. Lost during the entire interview, I only kept afloat by injecting some industrial jargon I had remembered from my earlier investigation. Think about how and why you could win or lose in these negotiations. Keeping a *"I can live with or without this job,"* attitude relieves a great deal of tension before any interview. Still, develop an interview attitude that expresses a sincere wish for employment in every meeting. Ask risky questions. Answer from left field. But hinting anything other than sincerity might cause some nasty responses.

Really impressed with a company? Be a little more conservative. Maybe take different approaches for each interview, because you may have different audiences. Be honest and complete. Know your strengths in order to emphasize them, and also your faults, so you can de-emphasize them. But don't pretend you have no weaknesses or faults.

One career counselor says, *"There is no bad job interview experience. Smart students will benefit from everything."*

You might even prepare you for the question most dreaded by recent college graduates, *"If you only had some experience I could hire you on the spot."* It will be the most antagonizing line of your entire job search:

> *"Well Mr. Doe—quite an impressive resume you have. All indications make you qualified for the job. Your salary expectation is no problem and references are excellent, but if you only had some experience... "*

Overcoming the *"no-experience barrier"* is difficult, but if you manage to substitute other work or school experiences for it, the world is your oyster! Interviewers will remember you. A Gonzaga University professor mentions, *"living in a dorm room while juggling a course load and being involved in extracurricular activities can mirror the 9-5 society."* Many recent grads feel likewise. One '86 grad points out,

> *"College serves as an excellent preparatory step for those who choose that path. College is all what you put into it. Taking basketweaving for four years will lessen the importance of a degree. Busting your ass for four years will give that degree a much greater value."*

It's as hard to change a boss's idea about experience being necessary as it is to change a professor's mind about your grade when you've skipped or slept through half the semester.

One aggressive interviewee explained her answer to this dilemma, *"I told them that was an unacceptable plea. I never had any college work experience, but look at my transcripts!"* Donald, a Georgetown University graduate stressed in an interview, *"I know I'm straight out of school with little experience, but my positive attitude far outweighs any drawbacks."*

Stress that you understand that you're a rookie and that all rookies make mistakes. But emphasize that you don't repeat the same mistakes twice. Tell how you deal with your errors. Mention that you do have a fair guesstimate of the 9-5 world. Tell them you're aware some coworkers will notice your blunders more than praise your achievements. Such statements reveal a surprisingly mature understanding of the 9-5 culture.

Often *"no-experience"* claim is an excellent scapegoat for real reasons. To fine-tune your style and discover true reasons for not getting an offer, call back interviewers and quiz them about the interview. Emphasize that you are requesting a critique on yourself, not the job possibilities. Sometimes circumstances prevent a company from extending a job offer. Try to find out why. Getting the real reason is no simple task because many regulations prohibit companies from revealing the true reason they chose not to hire you. But the real answer, if you can find it, may hold the key to getting you employed.

The charge of no experience demands a creative response. For example, use a business or drama group membership throughout college. Don't harp on personal accomplishments, but do stress the fact that you had to follow a routine, put in late hours without negatively influencing your grades and deal with all the people involved, without expecting or receiving money.

Convince your interviewer that college is not so different from the work world. Make your experiences worthwhile by researching the company and being very prepared.

The bottom line is knowing yourself and being able to see yourself in the job the interviewer describes. Project a positive picture to make the company want to hire you. Make them think that not doing so is their loss.

> *Project a positive picture to make the company want to hire you.*

One college recruiter replied, *"An interview can be the most honest representation of a college student's record. Resumes can be turned into perfection from dirt. An interview can make a person really reveal himself."*

Punctuality is important to interviewers. Occasionally, you will miss an appointment or have to arrive late. Do them the courtesy of calling. If they still don't understand, or don't want to re-schedule, don't even consider them a possibility. If they're like this while you're just interviewing, what do you think they'd be like if you were an employee?

Is it appropriate for me to ask questions?

Absolutely! Don't be afraid to scrutinize the company. Your commitment to a job can—and will—change your lifestyle. A company certainly won't be afraid to ask questions, so don't hesitate to do the same.

You must ask questions for your own information. Furthermore, your failure to ask good questions can be a bad mark on their report card of you. Most employers are highly skeptical of applicants who do not even have the wherewithal to try and gain some pertinent information concerning the nature of the position they are applying for and the facts on the company they propose to work for. Try consulting some working friends to discover what they wish they had known before taking a job. Ask some employers what types of questions impress them. Use good judgment in determining how and when to ask your questions.

Mr. Sundburg, from UCLA, stresses much of the transition problem initiates from this point: *"students don't do enough research...what they saw, was not there. Thus they leave...a good match between employer and graduate is everything."*

Base your interview questions on personal considerations such as money, advancement, time off, or company policy. Any issue that can affect your eventual performance is a topic for discussion.

As important as the issues you discuss is the order in which you discuss them. Starting off an interview by questioning the amount of vacation time is sealing your own fate. Flow with the interviewer.

It's better to ask, and find out that you don't want to be part of this company, than to wait until you've wasted six months being miserable. One ex-IBMer confessed she was so afraid of asking the wrong questions that she never got any answers. Don't swallow questions because the interview is going well or you're intimidated out of your skull.

Gene, an 1984 grad, told of such an instance.

> *"Since the company agreed to my starting salary, I refrained from asking about the second year's salary. Consequently, I'm going into my 20th month without any type of salary adjustment."*

Another graduate tells of how a boss was constantly hounding her. She explained that the money wasn't bad, but the work environment was horrible. Even though Kelly had nothing immediate lined up she admitted that she had *"had it up to here"* and finally quit. Kelly even ventured to say that no amount of money could make working with that boss bearable. Would more questioning on Kelly's part have prevented this from happening? Perhaps. Many recent grads are so anxious to gain employment that they close their eyes to obvious drawbacks in a position. Gathering more information doesn't guarantee a thing, but it does increase the odds of making a correct decision.

Your questions should be gauged to determine the desirability of a particular working environment. Compromising too much, at an early stage, between money and job satisfaction can distort one's work outlook for the next 40 years. The rookie 9-5er should probably pursue a more balanced situation.

Mr. Patrick Cave, an engineering veteran of more than 20 years, comments,

> *"Life is too short to be unhappy in a job if you can help it. Sometimes you have to grin and bear it, but a recent grad shouldn't have to stick in a position that he or she is unhappy in."*

Probing questions, asked in a professional manner, should not ruin your job search. You are considering spending 40 hours a week or more with a company; they should be willing and able to explain any issue you raise. One major college recruiter advises, *"read between all the lines to fully understand the job."* Beauty is sometimes only skin deep.

With small or private companies, explanations might be short since they can play by their own set of rules in answering questions. But you should be able to receive full and satisfactory answers to assure you that the company is stable. If you do step over the line in your questioning effort, don't be surprised if they respond by calling for the next applicant.

Don't get so caught up in your powers of persuasion and manipulation that you forget to discuss important topics. You're not always able to call later for answers; the phone is often never picked up off the hook. Be thorough in your questions, but not nitpicky. Referring back to a list kept in a neat folder is totally acceptable. Taking a folded up piece of paper out of your pocket is not advisable.

Why are there two, three, and sometimes four interviews?

Multiple interviews occur most frequently in situations in which employers have a multitude of highly qualified applicants to sift through. But they may also be a means for shrewd and careful employers to ensure their confidence in you. Multiple interviews enable an employer to test your validity. They determine if you dress, act, and respond the same way in each interview. By talking to you multiple times they allow more than one judge to participate in the decision making process. One interviewer might catch something that others missed. One employer told how his son revealed a potential employee's drug habit in their second interview. The father knew nothing about drugs, but the son was a recovering addict and spotted several traits immediately.

Even though interviews are costly, they are much cheaper than making an incorrect hiring decision. Be consistently better at each interview, for it will drastically improve your chances of being hired.

Can I do anything after an interview to better my chances of getting hired?

Evaluate your performance, but don't agonize over it. Prepare for your next interview. Using past experience for your upcoming trials is a good idea, but don't allow your misgivings about past performances to weigh you down or divert your direction.

One woman revealed how perturbed an interviewer became when she chewed a nail occasionally. She became so self-conscious about this habit that she only concentrated on not doing it and had to ask the interviewer to repeat many of his questions. Once it's over, it's over. Don't sulk, don't live it over. Second, write a thank-you letter to your interviewers. Thanking them for their time and consideration indicates your interest in joining their company. After completing this, all you can do is wait for their invitation, or their *"best wishes in your continued job search."*

What happens once I get the job offer?

Congratulate yourself but don't lose your head and immediately accept. Sit down and think. Talk it over with friends and people you know who work in that company or a similar field. Evaluate the pros and cons. Wait for other responses.

Most companies, however, have a time limit. Try to extend it if you can. Don't keep them in suspense, tell them you have other offers to consider.

Telling a company that you favor their offer might limit any bargaining power. Or it might allow you to get an extension in telling a company your decision. Perhaps the best thing is to tell them you've narrowed your choices down and must wait for responses.

Of course, they might withdraw their offer. If so, consider accepting this offer and forgetting about the others.

Brad, a recent grad from Pennsylvania, confronted this problem:

> *"An employer offered me a job one day after our first interview. He stunned me. I maneuvered to stall for time. Unfortunately, the time was insufficient. I wrote what I considered a great letter to gain additional time. His response was now or never. If I hadn't thought the company held great promise, I would have said sorry."*

Not revealing your decisions may entice a company to return another offer with additional benefits. This scenario is more likely for someone with more experience, however it's similar to when you were trying to impress a potential boyfriend or girlfriend. You started with maybe pizza and a movie, but might have to up the bidding to dinner and dancing if you really wanted to impress them.

Don't be shocked if the company makes an offer and sticks to it. Many companies play hard ball, but they can afford to. One American Greeting Cards recruiter stated, *"Very few college students have any room to bargain, but it all depends."*

What if I get a more attractive offer after having accepted a previous one?

Is there any such thing as a good headache? How about when several of your top choices offer you a job? It's just like pursuing more than one romantic interest at the same time. Usually, only one is interested, and sometimes not even one head is turned. It's really a problem when both decide to reciprocate. It's almost more trouble than it's worth.

Jane, a veteran 9-5er and a mother of two college students advises,

> *"Getting two offers at once can make college grads go crazy. They will get over-worried and think it's a life-or-death decision. No decision at an early age is that critical. It is confusing, but ever so complimentary."*

Being prepared for different outcomes is one precaution, but needlessly worrying over hundreds of different *"what if"* scenarios is ludicrous. Have different plans of actions ready. But, if you over do fore thought, it is nothing more than a waste of time.

If you accept an offer and then receive a more attractive offer from another company, is there really a dilemma? If there was a layoff, you'd likely be the first to go since you have little or no seniority. Changing your mind after you've accepted is not the worse thing you could ever do to a company. Better now than later. By getting out now, you are saving them time and money. Personal feelings could be hurt on both sides, but that's business. Don't worry that the firm will collapse without you, that is absurd. Will jumping ship reflect negatively on your record? Possibly, but being so new out of school may excuse the behavior. Proving such actions were the only sensible alternative can display a keen business aptitude. Make your explanations strong. If you stayed, you would always wonder *"what if?"*

Although sticking with your first offer might prove a very loyal gesture, it wouldn't be unusual for your performance and attitude to erode. Even family ties shouldn't keep you from changing your mind; you're the only one capable of managing your own interests.

If the first selection proves to be a mistake, pursue the other. Whatever the decision, decide to try your best. That's all that matters. It might not be satisfactory to an employer, but that doesn't matter. Not all jobs are meant for everyone. Even if all the preliminary steps were taken, some situations will not work out. If you tried your best, then you did your part.

Remember Robin? She changed careers three times in three years. Brian, from Chapter One, changed jobs a number of times following graduation—six to be exact. One study indicated that graduates will change careers seven times in their lifetime. Parents, old professors, and ex-bosses might accuse you of being *"immature, unrealistic and idealistic."* So what. Try a number of things, you'll be a wiser person for it. Don't be persuaded by others who think they know you better than yourself. They're wrong.

Sometimes you just have to say no to certain job offers and start all over again from square one. Even if you want to accept that first offer because you're sick of all the strenuous and tedious work you've done, don't take the easy way out.

One Ohio University grad suggests, *"Don't just take the first offer. If you get one, you'll get others."* There will always be more options opening up, even if it means settling for your bare minimum or less. Quite a few veteran 9-5ers and school officials argued that a new grad should take that first offer. Do you think they advocate marrying your first date?

Is there more to follow up on after I have accepted an offer?

Before you report to the job, verify all the details of the work arrangement. Then, check them again. It's your turn to experience all the trivial things that your parents complained about, such as vacation, personal leave, health benefits, salary, promotion, etc.

"*Yes, Mr. Doe, I accept your offer and will be there Monday morning for work.*" You have committed, but not irrevocably. People constantly change their minds in the 9-5 world. Now that you are a 9-5er, you can do the same. Become confident in your choice and prepare to give it a fair chance. Your feelings are important to your performance, but they are not etched in concrete.

There are many horror stories about 9-5ers who were recruited and hired under certain agreements but started with others. One 1984 grad told of accepting his first position at a bank with a starting salary of $16,000. When he realized his 52 weeks worth of paychecks would only total $14,600, he brought it to his supervisor's attention. She informed him it clearly was a misunderstanding on his part because $16,000 was impossible. He remembers thinking that if, as a waiter, he could keep beer orders for twenty people straight, he's not going to misunderstand $1,400 worth of salary. He asked her to check her records, but she claimed not to keep hard copies of that kind of correspondence. He was at a loss because he also failed to keep his documents.

Another trap that new 9-5ers fall into is that of company-assisted education claims. Many recent grads explained how they were told that their chances of returning for other degrees were very good. After several months, it became clear that educational costs would only be fully reimbursed after many years at the firm, and not a month before. Some companies explained that it's possible to get a master's, and just "*forgot*" the small detail of 15 years of service and naming your first born after the boss. Getting excited by a new job can sometimes cause one to overlook small details, which can become expensive lessons.

Maybe companies take the same liberties with their benefit claims as students do with their resumes. Feel brave and confident, take some steps to avoid this type of deception. Take whatever action you feel is appropriate, but realize you will be making waves. If you're going to disturb or object to company policy or claims, you had better be right, or prepared to suffer severe consequences.

We could blame the corporate culture, but let's put fault where it is due. Ever heard of *"caveat emptor"* (let the buyer beware). You are buying an employment package in exchange for your services. Your options might not be as open as others, but you have the final say. Check out the company. Call past employees, better business bureaus, headhunters, state employment commissions, or other public authorities.

One Richmond University graduate told of a simple strategy to avoid traps: *"Do what college taught you. Think critically before you decide."*

Should I broadcast my good fortune in having found a job?

Other people want to hear that you have a job. But be careful what you tell them and how you say it. Don't be a jerk. Lots of fellow graduates won't have jobs as good as yours, or even jobs at all. Don't rub it in that your job with XYZ firm starts at $25,000 per year, full benefits, tuition assistance, and a company car.

Put yourself in their shoes. Would you really like to hear someone else's good fortune when you've been rejected seven times in the last week? Certainly not. When you're telling people about your job, just mention it and let them ask questions.

A University of Tennessee grad told of an old roommate

> *"All he did was brag about his new job, his new condo and his new Porsche 944. At our next visit, he confessed that business had died except for one project that paid for his phone bills. I really wanted to shove my pay raise down his throat, but I kept my mouth shut."*

If you're not proud of your job, who has to know besides you? No one. If you are cornered into saying something, tell the curious that you're earning some good cash and getting some good experience. Adding that its rewards are pleasantly surprising can put some intrigue into the conversation. Maybe you'll discover some good points about the job if you're forced to defend it!

If, indeed, you've done well, let people be happy for you. Success changes some things, but not all. If you're in a crowd where all they like to do is brag about their jobs, you may want to exaggerate. However, if you feel that you might want to change jobs sometime in the future keep your network avenues open. It could be quite embarrassing to brag about a job and then have to question friends about whether their company has any openings.

Pass along information only if you feel confident. Likewise don't promise information you can't give to friends. Word of mouth is extensively used in business. It can be the sole reason for a big sale, a new hire or a gigantic failure.

In accepting a position don't forget to extend your network outside your profession. Jay's story shows the benefits. A 1987 grad, Jay started work at his engineering company at the same time as an old friend. Ten months later, both of them were fed up with their jobs. As you can imagine, they were in a predicament. But Jay had developed his contacts inside and outside of the company, while his friend's were limited to fellow employees. To help make the jump from his present job as a scientific analyst to stockbroker, Jay contacted friends from his alma mater. He landed a job after they helped him get interviews with several companies.

Meanwhile Jay's friend still works at the job he dislikes. Usually, people inside a company will not help you leave, while outside contacts may do everything in their power to assist. They have no ties or feelings of loyalty to the company, so their main concern is the individual. Jay advocates external socializing; it built him a network for his drastic career change.

Don't ever drop your network because you received an offer or already have a job. The need might unexpectedly arise one day. As discussed, networks can be used for more things than getting jobs.

Is the day before you start nerve-racking?

Many former 9-5 rookies described no preliminary fright until the night before. The last hours of freedom usually consist of dinner, some TV and notions of a good night's sleep to prepare for the big day ahead. Laying your head on the pillow you find you have never been more awake in your life. After three hours of tossing, turning and reading the ceiling, you finally fall asleep. Then you wake up 10 times during the next two hours fearing the dreadful sin of being late the first day. All those final night hours of staring at the ceiling are unnecessary. Relax. Act as if it were a normal evening until the eyes are shut solid.

One final word: if the job requires a change in sleeping habits, do it gradually rather than wait until the last night. The body needs several weeks to reset your internal clocks.

Your preconceptions of the first day activities may range from meeting with the company president for a fiscal policy discussion to lecturing the hospital's head nurse on proper sterilization methods. By afternoon you should be outlining possible improvements in the general corporate policy. The day's activities will end up at a new luxury office at 9pm reviewing personnel records. If, in fact, this occurs throw this book away.

How can I make a good impression on day one?

Most new employers won't expect too much in the first days. Aside from meeting coworkers you have to familiarize yourself with the environment, including that luxury office (the cubbyhole directly across from the snackbar).

At the outset, make sure you know where you're going and when the job starts. Surprisingly, too many rookies blunder by forgetting when to report to work. Perhaps it's nerves, but don't you do it.

One employer commented, *"If a person comes in late or appears sloppy on that first day, he or she is definitely starting out on the wrong foot."* One of the best things you can do is make a practice run to your job site before you actually start work. Being late your first day because you didn't take the time to figure out routes and traffic snarls is a capital mistake. Get a good idea of the general area and the amount of time required to go to work. Plan a couple of alternative ways in case of road problems.

One boss said, *"I hired a college kid who's got great potential, but he can't get out of bed in the morning. What does he think I'm going to do? I can understand being late occasionally, but eight out of your first nine days?"*

Many new 9-5ers have trouble getting into work. Pay attention to the details. Work habits can make or break your first days on the job. Little annoyances, such as being five minutes late, become more noticeable than the perceived strong suites you were hired for—particularly since you're not yet allowed to shine. Make your first impression the best.

One's personal appearance is as important as timeliness. Be aware of how others see you. Until you can showcase your skills and productivity, a boss will base his judgment of you on your work habits: energetic or lazy, willing or hesitant, friendly or shy.

The professionalism of your appearance will also register with your boss and your coworkers. Shorts, a tee shirt and a bandanna were acceptable dress in class. Completed assignments meant more than forgetting to shave for eight days. Not so in the 9-5 workplace. One such instance is recounted in one interviewee's story:

> *"I once received the raw end of an evaluation because I wore the same outfit two days in a row. I'd spent the night at a friend's house, and thought no one would notice a slightly worn suit. I was wrong. My supervisor noticed it first thing."*

No longer do grads play in the college environment. Graduation elevates one to the 9-5 major league. Borrowing a baseball expression: it's hardball time. Several 9-5ers expressed a strong desire to return to college for the three Fs: friendship, flexibility, and fun. Those times can be relived at certain points, but as a new 9-5er, one must realize that it is a totally different ball game now. Things merely snickered at in school could ruin a career. As you start to cash in on the benefits of college, you must leave its antics behind.

Chapter Six

THE FIRST 90 DAYS—
TEN COMMANDMENTS
FOR THE ROOKIE 9-5er

When you officially enter the 9-5 ranks, you find that few things are clear cut outside the simple math of the accounting department—and the people who crunch the numbers probably have some dissenting opinions about that.

At first, your situation may resemble what Maurice, from my alma mater, would describe as *"The Twilight Zone."* From trying to please the boss, to attempting to get service for the copy machine, to learning which company coffee room to use—all can be troublesome tasks to an inexperienced worker. It's an abrupt change from college.

You enter with pressures and prejudices against you. You will earn at least 30 percent more than those who didn't attend college, according to the U.S. Census Bureau. And bosses will be quick, sometimes severe, to disavow you of the notion that work—unlike some universities—is a place that will tolerate partying, nonsense or careless mistakes. You are a financial investment and a financial risk. Your company will try hard to get a maximum return from that investment, and it won't put up with attitudes or actions that could jeopardize its success. Some companies simply refuse to gamble with new graduates as one recent grad describes:

> *"Our company's policy is not to hire any new college grads. The bosses felt they were too far removed from understanding the problems of a new grad. There are too many adjustments for a new graduate to make any significant contributions."*

Certain attitudes towards new grads may catch you off guard. You will eventually maneuver with relative ease through the 9-5 work society. Still the initial course is frequently unmarked causing newcomers to stumble, fall or even collapse. Until you are able to develop and gain a sense of familiarity, abide by the following guidelines.

Are there any rules to follow that could help a new 9-5er?

Common sense will aid you in quickly adapting to your new environment. However, there are some pointers that could speed your adjustment. Specifically, gaining an insight into office politics is a good place to begin.

RULE #1: Office politics and office gossip can complicate the simplest tasks.

Frances Faulkenburg, an assistant VP of Student Affairs at Oklahoma State University explains, *"soon to be grads have misconceptions that everything will be explained and organized in detail, as in college courses. They don't understand office politics."* One interviewee explained her strategy in this manner: *"The only way to play office politics is from the sideline."* Imagine that your boss, or even a co-worker, shows you incorrectly how to use the office computer. You explain his error and he gets annoyed. Presto! You've made an enemy.

Things like this happen all the time. Many employers discount the contributions of new employees whether right or wrong. One veteran 9-5er warns, *"When some hot-shot college kid comes out swinging and makes an instant impact, it's often a co-worker's ambition to trip him up."*

As a new player in the 9-5 league, you should place achievement above company politics.

As a new player in the 9-5 league, you should place achievement above company politics. You may be astonished once you learn the power wielded by certain players in the game. Until you've been around a while, you will not know the particular sensitivities and idiosyncracies of your co-workers. It might be wise to try and maintain a field of personal neutrality until you gain better insight into the ins and outs of your particular office.

Interoffice politics gone awry can halt a company's operation. Imagine what they can do to an innocent newcomer who has inadvertently challenged the pecking order.

The pettiness of corporate politics can easily demoralize the most ambitious and talented new grads if they are not prepared for it. Often, interoffice tensions can arise from one person's efforts. One recent 9-5er stressed addressing those potential troublemakers before they get the chance to strike. It can result in a surprising outcome. He explained a personal incident:

> *"I remember a man who became very jealous because of my rapid advances. I thought for certain he would make waves. Before he had chance, I provided a list of names for his son to contact for a summer job. I had accidentally overheard him one afternoon talking about his son's summer predicament. I don't know if the list did any*

good, but this man's attitude towards me drastically changed."

One six-year 9-5 retail store supervisor says, *"Newcomers must understand that many veteran 9-5ers make themselves look good by making others look bad."* There's a little Washington DC in every office—you can't escape it. Try to understand who has the power and why it exists.

In some ways, it's not so very different from college politics. Favoritism is one factor which figures into almost any structured social environment. In college, certain professors favored certain students and it showed at grade time. Few people have not witnessed at least one incident in which favoritism led to the bedroom and sometimes the altar.

Some students became teacher's pets, gaining their rewards with highly visible classroom performance. Fellow students quickly identified them and tried to use them with such ploys as borrowing notes, volunteering for the same projects, or asking to get tutored. The office environment has its correlatives to these scenarios. The bosses of the 9-5 world have pets too.

Jack, a nine-year 9-5 veteran, describes a co-worker who *"became the boss's shadow. He started wearing the same clothes, started to smoke, and even bought the same type of car. It was ridiculous to watch, but it worked."*

You don't have to be the boss's pet to advance, but it's a good way to be recognized. Understand when a boss sees another imitate his personal habits, it might be somewhat of an ego boost. 9-5 players have egos like everybody else.

What are the consequences of engaging in office gossip?

A poor way to be recognized—and a serious snare of office politics—comes from participating in company gossip. Avoid gossip like the plague. Treat other people's mistakes as you want yours treated: silently. Corporate gossip is the 9-5 National Enquirer. Be particularly careful with personal information about your superiors. You may find that not knowing is the best policy. A friend of mine describes a situation in which her boss was engaged in a questionable office romance. At first, she was just as interested in picking up details as anyone else in the office. Eventually, she watched as co-workers suffered serious consequences from the boss's imagined or real perceptions of his employees' interests in his private affairs. She quickly made it her policy to close her ears to the whole thing. This made it much easier to keep her mouth closed as well.

People of all ages, occupations, and temperaments like to gossip—about each other, weekend activities or inter-office relationships. But it can turn innocent situations into full-fledged scandals. Every organization has individuals who like to keep the grapevine juicy.

Stories can stick to the teller, sometimes to their detriment. For instance, a new college grad in a management trainee program once indiscreetly proclaimed her unhappiness in a certain area of the company. She never thought to voice her opinion to her supervisor first. Instead, she bellowed it in front of the entire staff. The mistake stayed with her like a bad smell. Bosses do not take kindly to hearing of your dissatisfaction second hand.

At college, gossip was taken with many grains of salt. Gossip at work is much more dangerous. It can jeopardize promotion and, indeed, employment. If someone must talk, let them. But let the story stop with you. Be wary—you never really know who may be the source of the company grapevine. When I worked at a bank, I knew a very nice lady in personnel. I always thought I could confide in her. Luckily, I never did. Just before I left, I found out she was the biggest gossip in the company.

You may even find it helpful not to listen to gossip and hot topics at all. Many people have a way of making you an accomplice even if you only listen passively. Some people will even go so far as to trick you into affirming their opinions on a controversial topic so that they can claim you as a fellow dissenter. They may ask you, *"Don't you agree that the boss's policy on thus-and-so is completely unreasonable?"* When you answer (probably with complete indifference), *"Oh, sure,"* they may run to the boss with their complaint saying that you, for one, completely agree with their opinion. It happens.

A North Carolina placement advisor explained that college students don't understand the severity of the working environment because, *"college is a cushioned environment with different expectations."* Another senior placement advisor further explains why students are often shocked by the 9-5 politics: *"the university represents an environment somewhat isolated from the real world. Thus the student doesn't expect the work environment to be less forgiving."*

Many executives stressed the importance of refraining from participating. One comment best described their feelings: *"Exercise your ears all you want, but don't open your mouth."*

John, from the University of Chicago, states, *"the workplace is not a frat: you don't babble about everything. Doing such will cause some real problems."* A recent graduate of George Mason University who works at one of DC's most distinguished law firms observes,

> *"The gossip I hear is incredible. I was, and still am, amazed at how dangerous gossip can be if the wrong people hear it. Unfortunately, this possibility doesn't seem to ever stop people from talking."*

If caution with politics and gossip is important in most companies, it's essential when the business is family-owned. Often, gossip and politics seem to double or triple in intensity when family members work in the same company.

For instance, I once worked in a family-operated business. Although the patriarch's three daughters appeared to have little interest in the firm, I soon discovered I would have to yield my position if one of them married a man who did want to work for the company. The operation was theirs to do as they wish.

Colin, from the University of Scranton, employed in a family's business for three years since his college days advises, *"There's only one word that a college graduate need apply when entering a family business—neutrality. If you don't adhere to it, things will come back to haunt you."*

And how does your own personal life fit into the 9-5 picture?

Keep business and your personal life separate. Numerous employers consider this a cardinal rule. From your first interview to the day you retire, keep an ability to differentiate. Don't let personal matters interfere with business judgment. You might even quietly mention this ability during interviews or salary reviews. It's a skill that can open doors to a prosperous future.

"Good employees can leave their personal problems at the front door every morning. A person who seems to have a good balance in their work record and personal life usually does better than someone whose personal life is messed up," states Randy Turner, a 12-year veteran supervisor of the 9-5 scene.

RULE #2: Walk lightly and think twice before making waves.

When you start a job, many people in authority will make certain you realize that you're at entry level. Some of them perceive your skills and talents as a personal threat.

Passing people on your way up the corporate ladder can be very tricky, unless those people are also advancing.

Bret, a 10-year veteran in the manufacturing profession tells of a promotion that made him boss of the men who first hired and trained him: *"I'm going to step very carefully for a while because I need both men. It's a very weird feeling."*

Whether you pass people soon or not, remember that you are a new factor who might jeopardize a procedure, a job, or an entire department. Watch yourself and others carefully.

You can't blame the veteran 9-5ers. How would you feel if you put several years of concentrated effort into your job only to be rewarded with having to train the newest college brat, who knows everything, doesn't defer to experience, and may surpass you?

Worse yet, some think your genius or even your incompetence may put them out of a job. They are vulnerable. Changing careers at age 30, 40, or 50 is much more stressful than finding another school to accept your transcripts—especially if you have family mouths to feed. Each raise, or sale, or compliment you receive might have gone to them if you had not been hired. Understand?

Under these circumstances, the worst way to start is to pretend to know everything—especially since you don't. New 9-5ers make mistakes. Some are trivial, others epic in proportion. Either way, co-workers will notice and point them out to you. Thank them even if you don't want to. Be willing to accept and adjust to critiques and criticisms.

The company did not hire you for your state-of-the-art knowledge, and it won't mollycoddle you to get it. Whatever your potential, you still depend heavily on others just to reach a competent working level. Until that point, at least, eat humble pie and play the role of a thankful guest.

If the authority is your immediate boss, tread even more lightly. He can make you or break you. Supervisors are responsible for your evaluations. They present you to the rest of the company. As long as you remain under some authority's close scrutiny, be extra careful. Fulfill the requirements of the job and maintain the company image. Don't make waves. Be impartial to fellow employees.

A company will occasionally tolerate a minor offense—such as long coffee breaks—for a productive new employee. But a cocky new 9-5er who tries to get away with too much can be easily detected and penalized. Bosses may let things slide for a long while, and then lower the boom. If it happens to you, admit you're wrong and change. Don't complain.

Of course, a time will come when you can take advantage of unofficial company privilege. But abstain until you feel comfortable enough in the organization to participate with certainty. Learn the ropes before you skip them or you may swing from them.

If people are going to notice you, let it be for positive reasons—not for cockiness, policy violations or inappropriate flamboyance.

Are you saying I should never *"raise my hand"* to be noticed?

Heck no, but understand if you start slowly and inconspicuously, you lessen the jealousy factor against you. The less you appear to be out for singularly personal gain and recognition, the fewer road blocks you will confront.

Once you do something deserving positive recognition, make sure it gets noticed. All of your perfectly done work can produce nothing unless the appropriate people notice. *"Ringing in a big sale is always nice, but insuring that your sales manager hears is smart, as well as nice,"* notes Richard an '84 graduate now working as a phone-system salesman. *"Sometimes, it's not what you do, but who sees what you do that matters."*

Take the situation of two young reporters who have their stories printed on the front page for the first time. Both stories are equally well written. Only one reporter receives personal congratulations from the editor. Why? That one reporter made a habit of riding the elevator at the same time as the editor and sparking conversations with him. His name stood out.

The next day the editor decides a new reporter is needed for a specific story. The final two candidates happen to be the two reporters. Whom do you think gets the assignment?

Another effort you should make when appropriate is that of pointing out any collaborative accomplishments attained by you and your new colleagues. Your successes will in no way be diminished by acknowledging gratitude for another's assistance or guidance. Teamwork and collaboration is essential to any successful business venture, operation, or activity. Demonstrating an ability to work well with other people can never be anything but an asset.

What about a situation in which you have to speak up against a fellow employee or a harmful policy?

Do it, but handle yourself calmly and professionally.

Another example of using exposure to your benefit is that of two management trainees sentenced to the Xerox room for an entire day. Both are upset about this misuse of their college skills. At the end of the day, both return to their boss to distribute their work. One trainee complains bitterly about Xeroxing all day. The other mentions several possible improvements to the Xerox room. Which trainee will be most favorably remembered?

Eventually blending in with a group of co-workers can make the vultures and irate bosses give up—either because new prey has been hired, or you've escaped their reach. This can save your life by giving you a good vantage point for gaining helpful hints of what lies ahead. You may find a few whom you can trust enough to let off steam. But stay wary, discreet and alert to backstabbers even then.

RULE #3: Deadlines are reality, and time is money.

"Extremely strict time requirements are often the cause of your so called 9-5 Shock," notes Russell, an '83 graduate of East Tennessee State. *"Time is no longer yours to do with as you wish."*

Unlike college, the corporate world has no concept of *"free Fridays"* and incomplete or ignored assignments. It tolerates little. In fact, even 9-5 is not a given. It might be 9-8 and sometimes weekends.

"Acceptable excuses for abusing or neglecting work hours don't happen too often," says one Honeywell executive. Accept this as the gospel truth. Your habits might need some coercing for the first months, but you eventually adapt. Don't allow a lackadaisical attitude prevent you from ever experiencing day #91 of the first job.

Unlike college you cannot borrow notes from a colleague, or count on your absence not being noticed. Newer and fresher graduates who would be happy to take your place are always available. Graduation causes some students to imagine their BMWs and three martini lunches await them. Even if it does, it's still not without the price of time commitment.

Many 9-5ers describe days off or early leave as scarcer than hen's teeth. Weekends were free in college to stay on campus, visit a friend's school or go home. There were also people willing and eager to join you, as long as there were no exams the Monday following. Be prepared to forfeit these road trips. You'll still want to go on adventures, but you are no longer the determiner of the length of a weekend. *"Skipping an occasional Friday, Thursday, or even, a Wednesday was really no problem,"* explains Jim, a 1987 grad from Texas A&M. *"But if I tried to skip out on my boss there would be a problem of no income for the next week."*

The company's ownership of your weekday time also implies that you don't come to work hungover or too tired to perform. When you accept your first job you automatically refuse all-night bashes, unless you—unlike almost everyone else—can erase the effects by 6am the next morning and remain fresh and efficient for the remaining 8 hours. There's little room for appeal or leniency, because others' work depends upon yours. Companies require efficient teamwork for production and profit. Hungover party animals are not "cool," they are a financial drain and a drag.

What's more, unlike your college class and study schedule, working hours are often a fairly inflexible 9-5. You probably can't scatter them around the week, day and night, for your convenience. Veteran 9-5ers get as annoyed at having to stay beyond 5 p.m. as you did when a professor tried to keep one class late when your next one was at the other end of campus. In the working world many people might have families waiting for mom or dad's return. Respect their time. Not everyone lives on frozen dinners.

"Only a student who has had a summer job, a co-op, or an internship will really understand these circumstances," notes a Florida Institute of Technology advisor. John, a recent 9-5 entrant agreed *"being the king of internships prevented me from*

being surprised by any changes from the college life. So many of my friends were wiped out by the strict time restraints."

The 9-5 schedule is also more repetitive than college. Could you imagine going to the same class every day of the week for more than three hours—freshman English for 250 straight days? Sometimes the working world can be paralleled to just such a scenario.

Should college have better prepared you for this radical revision of your concept of time? Two arguments exist. The first view—voiced by many in the corporate world—says that since employers demand strict daily contributions, colleges should too. The second view, held by many educators, sees college as a proving ground in which students themselves are to seek out responsibilities and mature into young adults. As one professor put it, *"We are not going to become babysitters."*

Whatever you think college should have done, the realities of work are not likely to change. So accept them, take the benefits of work with the bad, and don't waste time worrying about what you can't control.

RULE #4: Being new in the 9-5 game gives you an allowance for mistakes, but you can't fail repeatedly. Learn from your mistakes.

Being new in the 9-5 world gives you some allowance for mistakes, but you can not fail repeatedly—you can not become a liability. Good employers let new grads have ample opportunity to make the preliminary transition. The company discovers the talents and weaknesses it has hired. Likewise, for you, the first few months are a chance to discover your own weaknesses and respond appropriately.

Since many good businesses take time with new employees to evaluate their potential use, this is also an opportunity to consider whether or not you want to stay with the company. Mark McCormack states in his bestseller *What They Didn't Teach You at Harvard Business School* that the best companies (or employers) will take *"five hours to teach you something they could do in five minutes."* Staying on with a business is a two-way street. Is the company treating you correctly? Likewise, are you yielding the company a fair profit on its investment?

If a company seems to be unfairly expecting results *"yesterday,"* it may indicate an unhealthy attitude toward employees. Examine their expectations. Are they acceptable? Do they seem achievable? If not, this company might treat you to a severe 9-5 shock.

If you're patient with your company's progress, they should extend the same courtesy. One employer commented on the progress of her new hire, a 1987 grad, by saying, *"It's been a long time coming, but he can do it now."*

The 9-5 society bases much of its work flow on the *"one-shot"* principle. Don't panic! Causing the Xerox machine to jam won't put your head on the chopping block. Even being the sole cause of a $1,000 mistake won't halt your employment if you're working for a smart company. Only when the mistake really plunders the corporate coffers will the best companies send you back to the want ads. Believe it or not, companies are expecting their new investment to *"screw-up."* An employer once advised, *"If you know-it-all college kids don't make mistakes, then it's an indication that you are not trying."*

Unlike college, the corporate world has a bias against repeated blunders.

The academic world incorporates a large safety net throughout your schooling. Even the most critical areas (grades and entrance exams such as the C.P.A. or L.S.A.T.) include room for failure. *"Screwing up"* either requires retaking the test or the class. Unlike college, the corporate world has a bias against repeated blunders. The chances for redeeming yourself are neither as quick nor as easy as recovery from a bad semester. Nor is it as simple to convince an interviewer—whose job may hang on your performance—to give you a second chance.

One small businessman sums up a common attitude when he says, "*It's my job to pay my employees. It is their main responsibility to contribute to the company's cause. Not following this means the end of the payroll checks.*"

RULE #5: Companies no longer close their eyes to after hours activities.

Play by the company guidelines. In the era of random drug tests, what you do in your spare time is no longer strictly your own business, and consequences can be harsh. Recently, for example, Houston passed a law permitting immediate dismissal of city employees who test positive for illegal drug traces.

Ask Michael a 1985 University of Connecticut grad, how easy it is to ruin a promising career. The day after he got high for the first time in 15 months, he found out his company had opted to reinstate random drug checks. What's more, in this case, it was a direct effort to pare down the work force. He avoided the ax only through pure, unlikely luck: he was repairing the company doctor's car. The doctor promised to cover for Michael—that once—in exchange for the mechanical work.

Bill, a 1987 grad and coke user, thought he had a job locked up with his uncle's company. In fact, his uncle had even congratulated him. He had a hit the day before the entrance physical to thank for his rejection letter. His uncle says it's the only reason Bill wasn't hired.

Drug problems are growing increasingly serious for companies, and they are paying more and stricter attention to potential abuse. Large programs are being instituted to rid the workplace of drugs. Although it might not appear to be as prevalent, drugs are often as widespread in the office as on the college campus. Participating is foolish for some companies are now considering using NARCS. Being caught will likely mean termination. One company's personnel executive revealed that if any prospective employee's background indicates drug use, it means automatic disqualification for the job. One bright aspect about the spread of drugs is the growth of drug-help programs. Many companies are very willing to help financially, if a person voluntarily seeks assistance.

Even alcohol, though much more socially accepted, faces increasing scrutiny. Drunken behavior after working hours will be remembered. If may not mean your last-ever day on the job. But rest assured: you'll be one of the bumbling ex-rookies whose name will be fondly remembered at the coffee station.

RULE #6: Do as you are told; don't allow your ego to get in the way.

Another risky intoxication to have is awe of your own talent.

"A great deal of college grads get off to a bumpy start because of their ego," notes Joe, a veteran 9-5er for more than 20 years at Unysis.

> *"If they would only do what they are told and not what they imagine their degree merits. If many of you would just deflate your egos and let the education speak for itself, the transition would be much easier."*

This attitude can be found widespread amongst many veteran 9-5ers.

Beginning a job should humble anyone. You will require many more favors than you can promptly return. You start out ignorant of everything from sick leave policy to the location of the restroom nearest your office. You're going to have to ask other people for answers—just as if you were a freshman again.

Keep in mind, few first positions are really interesting or fulfilling in view of your long-term career objectives. It's only a start. Those college grads who can accept entering at the bottom, no matter how may degrees they have, what GPA they carried, or what fraternity they belonged to, and still understand their potential and long range goals will excel in any organization.

Your best strategy is a simple one. Use the basics and only the basics. Know how to listen. Speak when spoken to.

Be willing to do whatever is asked of you. And be able to write correctly.

Don't be like the rookie newspaper reporter. Shortly after being sent out on an interview, his boss received a call from a police officer friend asking him who this young guy was who kept screaming that all relevant information had to be given to him because he was from the Gazette.

His boss says, *"I almost died when I heard what that rookie reporter was saying. Now you know why employers hesitate to hire a lot of rookies!"*

A personal classic was my decision to show a boss I could sell any piece of junk merchandise. Instead of seeking advice concerning the value of an old revolver, I convinced myself that I knew enough to make the decision. I sold that gun for what I thought was a premium price. After bragging to my boss of my great sale, I was informed *"Jerry, I just refused an offer three times that amount. How many times have I told you to ask if you were unsure!"*

Protect yourself against the 9-5 pitfalls. Sometimes all you have to do is to follow directions. Until you prove an ability to handle the simple situations, many 9-5 veterans will refuse to jeopardize you or themselves. Live by the "KISS" (Keep It Simple Stupid) principle while breaking into the 9-5 league. Triple check assignments, and refuse temptations to strut your perceived stuff by straying from assignments.

The corporate game can get you coming and going. Observe carefully. Listen very closely and do what is asked of you to keep the first months tranquil. Less attention in many early transitions is better than calling attention to yourself. During your first few months, your position is one that will be critiqued. The less criticism, the faster your progress.

Exposure may be the key to progress, but don't pursue it too hastily, for it carries a price tag. It's often wise to start inconspicuously. If nothing else, it can divert jealousy away from you and please bosses who want you to stay with them for awhile.

Similarly, it's wise not to flaunt your education. All the education in the world can never fully substitute for practical experience. And even though college may have been the best time of your life, remember that many highly intelligent co-workers or superiors never had the chance to attend. You may be a painful reminder of what they missed. Don't expect people to want to hear your stories about school, particularly boastful ones. Besides, resting on your college laurels may lead you to do a lot of resting at home looking at the classifieds.

RULE #7: Determine a proper time balance between work and play.

It doesn't take a lot of discussion for most of us to realize that adopting a *"work, work, work"* and no play attitude makes Johnny (or anybody else) a very dull boy (or girl). The more you enjoy your free time, the more productive and happy you are on the job. It's that simple.

Find more than one way to enjoy your free time. If the only thing that interests you outside the office is windsurfing, what happens when the marina is only open on weekends, you work Saturdays, and it rains on Sunday? Despair, disgruntlement, and disappointment on the job.

But if you also enjoy such things as movies, museum exhibits, plays, horseback riding, jazz, dance, and night classes, you're much better off.

Try to understand that too much work hampers any play, and too much play certainly hampers work: even the appearance of too much play can spoil others' opinions of you.

Again, the rule invites comparison to college. You have a new set of priorities to put in perspective. The adjustment is not easy. But it is a must.

RULE #8: You must work well with associates you didn't choose yourself.

In the 9-5 world, the boss decides who spends time together. You're only free outside of work. The workplace is much like sports. Once drafted, a rookie gets thrown into team with a group of unfamiliar people. He must fit in or be cut.

In the 9-5 world, companies require everyone to cooperate so the company can prosper. The protection of being the new college kid may smooth over a few wrinkles at first. But the parasitic behavior of college (such as resting on the laurels of whomever did all the work for the research group) is usually not tolerated in the 9-5 society because money is involved. If you're not a team player by nature, fake it quickly and believably, or you will struggle.

Throughout your transition you will be exposed to all levels of management. Understand each situation in which you will work. How? Ask questions. Being a recent grad brings many headaches, but it also allows many alibis in doing things an experienced employee might not even consider. Use that title of *"new hire"* to the fullest, because it only lasts so long.

You'll learn quickly that you can't approach every relationship the same way.

You'll learn quickly that you can't approach every relationship the same way. Admittedly, you must consistently act bright and professional, but beyond that, each group of colleagues demands a different style.

With top managers, it's not appropriate to tamper with their decisions. That doesn't mean you can never show individuality, but it does mean an attitude of joking or familiarity seldom sets well in their presence. Don't think you're on the same level as they are just because they're talking to you. Follow the lead of your immediate boss. If he's formal, keep your coat buttoned and your tie straight, and if he's casual, loosen up a bit. In working with the *"big boys"* do exactly as you are told as long as it doesn't violate your personal morals.

Be careful with middle management, too. Be able to tell them with a smile on your face that you love making copies for three straight hours. Middle management might be your biggest threat to advancement—you're a rival in the long term. Since everyone can't be at the executive-level, many individuals stall at middle management. It's then possible for younger employees to pass them. Aggravating a superior will give them every reason to prevent you from ever having the opportunity to advance to the executive branch, or for that matter the middle level. One rookie explained that she received a terrible evaluation from her supervisor because she solved a computer-report problem during her first days in the department. She's sure that she got that evaluation because the department vice president congratulated her, but questioned that supervisor's capability.

In working with operations personnel, you should generally treat people as they treat you. Superiors will help you develop proper relationships and management styles in each sphere. If one style doesn't work, try another. If you can use many different management styles, you will be more useful, respected, and valuable.

It would be plain silly to think that you will get along with all the different personalities that you will encounter. At college, you were allowed to ignore or avoid others. Not so in the 9-5 world. From the viewpoint of superiors, your taste or preferences don't matter at this stage of the game. Until you prove your worth, be able to work with whomever, whenever, or whatever. Honestly, you have no choice.

RULE #9: Patience is a workplace prerequisite.

By your senior year in college, you had already proven yourself in many ways, and it showed in your attitude. But an inexperienced freshman with your *"I've paid my dues"* attitude would face some painful lessons. Similarly, you are unproven as a player in the 9-5 world. As a corporate freshman, you cannot rush headlong into uncharted territory and expect to fare any better than the ignorant college freshman. Albert, from Sam Houston State, recommends a smart approach, "by all means a new person should stay patient and keep an open mind."

It may seem that the only thing worse than adjusting to the different pace, schedule, and social pattern of working life is realizing that your boss is letting your valuable talents go to waste. Imagine your company as a dog sled team. One dog may be much faster, but he must run at the others' pace.

Of course, it's better to have the boss tell you to relax than to be told to speed up. I remember my boss informing me that I was good with the big problems but was horrible at ironing out the little details. Never before were details so important. If I didn't slow down and change my habits, I was told I would be penalized. Consequently I changed—and fast!

Quality, not quantity, is a key to a good start.

Another point to evaluate is whether your personality and work habits may be too much for some companies to handle. Although many new college grads cannot fully comprehend that working environment, you need not be blind to the writing on the wall. Square pegs can't fit into round holes, but they can be molded and shaped so that they one day might work. Determine a timetable for a company's molding process. If their time frame and your's seem to fit together within reason, stay with it. If not, analyze the situation. If changes on both sides cannot be agreed upon, pick up the Sunday classifieds.

Looking back, you realize the last semester of school flew by—as you rushed to meet deadlines, hurried to cram for exams, flew across campus to get to a class on time. You've rushed for four years. Then you were hired by a business firm, and now you're doing the exact opposite (some graduates do get their talents put to the test immediately, but most do not).

When you start in the working world, a boss might ask you to slow down to a snail's pace, and learn through absorption, as if you were a sponge! Feel flattered that the boss wants to invest extra time (and money) on your development.

The length of time you spend imitating a sponge varies from company to company. Since college graduates are supposed to be quick learners, you might only get two or three days to get the stuff under your belt. Most large or established companies, however, require you to complete a long training session. One recent grad working as a manager trainee for Hertz Rent-A-Car, comments:

> *"The most important aspect about a first year of work is becoming familiar with working rather than going to classes. A great deal of learning will be through osmosis."*

You may feel bored to death squandering your educated brain at the copier or on the telephone. Remember that bosses sometimes test your patience and commitment before entrusting bigger responsibilities to your care. Remember that at college you had to spend several semesters taking general courses before they let you go on to the interesting ones.

Greg, a 1983 MBA grad, experienced this waiting game with patience:

> *"My management training really tested my patience. I used to think of all my schooling and ask myself—for what? But I saw others who stuck it out now have very good positions in the company."*

If the wait becomes intolerable, speak to superiors about your impatience. There are only three things that can occur:

- Your concerns will be addressed.

- Your problem remains unresolved.

- Your superior will inform you *"that's tough, continue or leave."*

Always be willing to accept the worst case scenario. Do not be foolishly unprepared to handle any and/or all consequences.

What was better: an A in one course or a 3.7 GPA for the entire four years of college? Which is more impressive to a professor? First jobs—and, more so, first months of those jobs—may be paralleled to a one course shot. Pursue that career GPA; it will benefit you and impress potential bosses.

RULE #10: Bosses are right, even when they are wrong!

Unlike college, your bosses often supervise you closely, hold you to strict accountability, and don't walk out of your life every 16 weeks. Do 9-5 veterans—far removed from their own college days—feel a bumpy transition is one of the dues 9-5 rookies must pay to fully respect the working world? Inevitably some do. Unfortunately, there isn't a darn thing you can do about it. Upon selecting a job, I can only hope a great emphasis is placed on what future boss impressed you the most. Your upcoming boss *"holds all the cards."* Pick one that plays fairly.

Is a younger boss better? Do older bosses sympathize with grads? Age does not seem to be a determining factor. Character flaws know no age limits. In questioning several students regarding who was to blame for a tough transition, some of them mentioned their bosses. Many others, though, said bosses had little to do with a tough start and put the burden on themselves.

What is a boss looking for in a new graduate?

One small business owner says that any college graduate who can free up a supervisor's time proves her worth. If you've graduated from college, employers assume that you've earned it, that you're responsible and intelligent. Accept responsibility for your own career development if you want to be thought of as a professional. A concerned boss will try to guide you, but meet him more than halfway and avoid questioning your boss's authority.

Many employers blame new graduates for thinking the book's way is the only way and failing to realize that most situations are not as clear-cut as they appear. They want you to be creative and show an ability to see the gray as well as the black and white.

One employer said *"college graduates are programmed for right or wrong answers."* He gave a personal example:

> *"I had a new grad training to run several of my route salesmen. One salesman was never hitting quota. He told me that there was no alternative but to fire him. According to a book, that would be the right answer. However this salesman is related to my very valuable secretary. The 9-5 workplace has many hidden scenarios that can pose difficult dilemmas for recent grads. With time and experience, a recent grad can correctly handle these situations. Right out of school, I would not think so."*

Companies and bosses who can afford to give you the time to adapt are investing more and more in development. Since this extra investment also carries a greater risk, show them you respect their training. If employers perceive a negative attitude, beware of serious repercussions. Neglecting other's efforts will hamper your continued advancement.

Can you argue with a boss?

First, learn your supervisor's ropes and guidelines. Know what impresses and aggravates him. Know when to speak up and when to shut up. Many bosses say they would like to see college grads learn to provide better input and critical perceptions. Even an occasional, calm, polite debate is not taboo—if you know both your boss and your subject well and can accept whatever the final decision is. Most bosses agreed that new grads have good concepts, but the rookies don't always communicate their ideas well.

These rules of thumb for making suggestions to a boss will help:

1. Know the operation or procedure that you're discussing.

2. Know whom it may affect.

3. Outline possible outcomes and effects, especially the negatives.

4. Make your suggestion at the right time, in the right manner.

5. Make sure you'll be there to help make the idea work.

The more complete your suggestion is, the better you look. If you have doubts about your idea, keep your mouth shut or mention it only to someone you respect as knowledgeable in the subject. Don't be labeled the big talker who starts with nothing and ends with nothing, but sounds good throughout.

A good working relationship grows from mutual respect and understanding. A boss, surprising as it may seem, may well recall what you are experiencing. And since he has dealt with new hires—and you have not—he may have a broader, more experienced outlook on whether he's really being fair to you. Flexible bosses are rewarded by grateful employees. But some bosses, admittedly, are not. Inflexible situations are often costly to all parties concerned.

Brian, from Chapter One, recalls:

> *"My boss kept tightening his time restrictions until lunch hours became the exception rather than the rule. I felt guilty trying to get time off for a doctor's appointment. My boss kept giving me more and more responsibility without any compensation other than the paycheck. Finally, I quit. She still has no idea why I quit. I know that the business relationship is one of give-and-take, but the balance was too uneven."*

At first, the strain between a rookie 9-5er and a veteran boss can be severe. One former 9-5 rookie, now a boss himself blames many employers, *"Many bosses are too far removed from their college days to understand."* However, many employers criticize new graduates for expecting too much too soon. Strong feelings by each can cause sincere efforts to reach a mutual understanding to disappear. Don't allow this—working relationships are a key to success. Remember that you were hired to make the boss's job easier and save him time and effort. Bosses don't have a lot of time. They try to locate responsible people to perform regular duties so they can concentrate on the big projects.

Any final suggestions?

Keep all of the foregoing advice in mind. Be sensitive to the uniqueness of any situation you may find yourself in. Whatever obstacles you confront, be clever and creative in addressing them. Draw upon your own experience, the advice of others, and any intuition or insight you might be blessed with. Stay on top of your situation at all times. Sometimes being on top may mean keeping a low profile. Sometimes it will require making your presence known. Be wise enough to recognize the determining factors and strive to anticipate all possible repercussions to any actions on your part.

Chapter Seven

UNCERTAINTY IS A CERTAINTY

The preceding chapters dealt with strategies for coping with some of the less than desirable aspects of entering the working world. Any new job, any new phase of your life, will require adjustments of you. But what happens when the bad seems to far outweigh the good?

As soon as the thought of quitting your first job creeps into your brain, an internal struggle will ensue. At first you will probably only half-heartedly toy with the thought—you may not view quitting as a real, feasible option. For many, the thought will stop at this stage. For others, the idea which originally appeared ludicrous—the option which you only jokingly allowed yourself to indulge in—will suddenly become a viable option. That is, at least one part of you will seriously consider quitting. Another side of you will begin indulging in self-loathing at the mere thought of such irresponsible behavior. *"How can I possibly consider quitting a job I should feel lucky to have?"* So, you enter a new phase of the 9-5 shock.

Is it bad to second-guess your first job decision?

By no means. However, there will be plenty of people to make you feel guilty for being *"irresponsible," "ungrateful," "rash and impatient,"* and *"immature"*—the list may go on and on. The truth is, some of these accusations may actually apply to you and your disenchantment with your first job. Then again, they may not. Considering other options is no crime, but be certain of your decision before any actions are carried out.

Is it common to consider quitting so soon after being hired?

For recent graduates, yes. As noted earlier, according to one study between 40 and 50 percent of new graduates actually do quit their first job within the first year. Think how many more must at least consider quitting.

The reasons recent grads are prone to first job regrets are endless, but several circumstances are commonly found in a new grad's explanation.

1. Money—not enough
2. Personality conflicts
3. Lack of free time
4. Lack of responsibility, or challenge

It seems as though the latter is the most common reason amongst first year grads.

The symptoms of that worrisome ailment known as *"job displeasure"* may progress like this. You begin feeling reasonably comfortable with your surroundings. But, you are, nevertheless, hoping for more challenging duties than operating the postage machine. Your current position is euphemistically referred to by supervisors as *"your building block."*

But when your building block begins to take on the appearance of a permanent and inert fixture, you become anxious. You begin to feel like Willy Loman in Death of a Salesman. From deep within you comes the cry, *"But I have a college degree!! This job is not me!!"*

Often the cause of uncertainty comes simply from an inability to understand where you are in relation to where you are going down the 9-5 road. And, again, you may have come out of college without accurate foresight into the 9-5 world.

A great number of grads feel this way about their job at one point, so don't feel guilty or try to deny the truth of your feelings. Problems of adjustment can be dealt with in an open, professional manner if you are giving the company your best and don't complain constantly or dwell on trivial things. You may be unhappy with the job itself; on the other hand, you may just be unhappy with certain aspects of the working life that will be a part of almost any situation you find yourself in.

Arguments for staying

If you are thinking living or staying with your job, consider the advice of one Fortune 500 recruiter:

> *"College grads must convince themselves to give that first job a fair shot. It's similar to a school that might not be one's ideal college. But a full two years will allow a student to get all the preliminary classes out of the way. Sticking with the first job for more than two months, if nothing else, allows a new grad time to adapt to the real world."*

Martin, a middle manager for a Big Eight accounting firm, observes *"For young grads to expect to be happy or satisfied every day is an idiotic line of thinking. Restlessness can often represent ambition."*

Many people suggest giving a new job at least a year to pan out. Reasons for such a wait include allowing time for you and the company to get to know one another and improving your job marketability. For some arbitrary reason, one year seems to be viewed as the magic number here. The idea is that future prospective employers will be less likely to view you as flaky and fickle if you can say that, while you were not happy with your first job from day one, you chose to stick it out so as to be absolutely certain that your dissatisfactions were merited and not the product of some temporary set back. You should also be able to give good, reasonable, and well thought out reasons for having left.

However you choose to play your cards, give some thought to how you will answer inquiries into your short-lived first job. You need to be able to account for your actions to future potential employers without casting yourself in a negative light.

How do I decide between riding it out and moving on?

Deciding to quit may relieve much tension and lead to an exciting, fresh beginning. Then again, deciding to stay may prove to have hidden rewards. Working through the questions below will help you decide on a wise course of action.

1. **Do you have another job lined up?**

   If you do not, you may have to jump at the first offer. Since bills must be paid, can you get a job with flexible hours to keep interviewing hours free? Do some serious thinking. Going down an unknown road is more difficult than a well mapped one.

2. **Would the job be better in a different place?**

   Is it better to work in a city or on the beach? Are the bosses the problem? Is it the salary or benefits? Perhaps you want a job with different duties altogether. Or, maybe the problems are related to the place of employment rather than the actual job description. Remember that few jobs will be perfect.

3. **Are you unrealistically assuming that the grass must be greener somewhere else?**

   Don't listen to your friends talk about their jobs. They might be lying. Even if they are perfectly happy—are you sure the things that make them happy will make you happy? Base your decisions on your own situation, not on covetous thoughts for another's job or the picture they paint of it.

4. **Are you in the job for experience?**

   If so, and you feel like you are getting it, seriously consider sticking with it. Put up with the nonsense for a little longer. Imitate a sponge and absorb as much as you can. Set a time limit if you must, and tell yourself it will only be eight hours a day for a few more months.

5. **Are you familiar with the job you want next, and do you have the contacts and resources to get you there?**

   Let good people advise you. Anytime you try something new, or test untried areas, you risk all the security you've built up. Don't head for the front line until you are ready.

Evaluating the options

Every decision involves an evaluation of pros and cons. You go through such an evaluation process on a very informal level when you are choosing between McDonalds and Burger King, for example. But, for more weighty decisions, you will want to contrast and compare the options most meticulously. Remember this, in any decision-making situation, no matter what you choose, *something will be lost and something will be gained.* Decisions inherently require some type of trade off—otherwise, they would not be so agonizing. If you are lucky, you will lose nothing of any consequence. However, in most cases, there *will* be aspects of the rejected option that you will miss or regret. Rarely does life allow us to *"have our cake and eat it too."*

Are you saying it's a no win situation?

No. You can still come out on top. It's a matter of deciding what price you are willing to pay for what benefits.

It is your job to ensure that your wins exceed your losses. Remember as well that what we view as gains and what we view as losses are very personal perceptions. You decide what you can afford to lose and what you refuse to forego.

Accept that you are unlikely to find a situation which is completely satisfactory.

Know all of the assets and all of the drawbacks for each option you are considering. Accept that you are unlikely to find a situation which is completely satisfactory. We *are* talking about work here. Even the lucky few who absolutely love their jobs will admit to some wearisome task or situation which casts a shadow on their duties.

A career change has far reaching implications which can affect every aspect of your life. Do not enter such decisions lightly.

As you make your decision, be certain that, in your readiness to get out of a bad situation, you are not setting yourself up to walk right into another one. There will be down-side aspects to any choice; know what you expect to gain from the choice you make and what you will have to pay for those gains. Once you have made a choice, be prepared to accept the bad with the good. The best way to do this is to stretch your brain and imagine all of the possible perks and pitfalls of every option you are considering. You are probably aware of a decision-making method in which you make a two column list which contrasts all of the pluses and minuses of a proposition you are considering. This might be a good time to put this technique to work.

Go ahead and sit down with at least one sheet of paper. You may choose to use two, devoting one to your current job and the other to a job you are considering, or unemployment, or the job you believe you *should* and *could* have. You may deem it appropriate to analyze only your current job since the proposition of quitting often represents a complete unknown. After all is said and done, you may favor the known, with all its drawbacks, over the unknown which is a complete gamble.

Remember that the *number* of negatives or the *number* of positives should not be your primary concern. It is important that you consider your list in terms of which perks you really value and to what extent you can endure the negative aspects of each proposition. You may want to use a method of qualifying each entry. For example, you could rate all of the positive aspects on a scale from one to ten with ten representing a compensatory item which you value greatly and would be extremely hesitant to give up. Items rated with a "1" may be favorable items which are, nevertheless, practically inconsequential to you. For example, even though you may consider the proximity of your office to your apartment to be *technically* good, you may not be so opposed to commuting that you would be willing to give up something you truly value for this convenience.

Accordingly, rate the negative aspects from one to ten with ten representing any factor you find virtually unendurable. *"Ones"* would be only minor frustrations—the sort you might find any where. On both sides, each item could be rated according to its importance to you, with tens representing both the extreme good and the extreme bad.

However, *do not get carried away in quantifying your happiness and unhappiness*. Certainly, such a procedure is not an exact science. Some things may be so important to you that you can not put a number value on them and you will not really care if the down-side aspects total much higher than the one "10" you are holding out for. Just remember that each item in each list should be considered specifically in context of your relationship to the situation. Remember also to (1) consider absolutely everything, (2) to think in terms of trade-offs, and (3) to think about the long-term future implications of each proposition.

Imagine a woman who has recently required a high pressure job in a working situation she finds dehumanizing and miserable for numerous reasons. However, the money is pretty good and the possibility for advancement is very promising. In fact, it is a fairly high status job. But, she loathes her job. She goes home in misery every day and even in her leisure hours she finds herself completely occupied with concerns over her job. The innocent query from friends, *"So, how's the job?"* is enough to get her started on a virtual dissertation describing the many new agonies which have entered into her day-to-day existence. This woman, we'll call her Mary, has the opportunity to return working as a full-time staff member with the same department she did student scholarship work for as an undergraduate. Here, she would love her job and her colleagues; but, she is concerned about the lack of advancement potential. Also, staying on a little while longer in her current position would greatly increase her future marketability while the job at the university would be slightly less impressive to future prospective employers. Mary's list might look something like this:

ARGUMENTS FOR BANK:

- Salary exceptional for entry level position.

- Advancement potential is great.

- Experience extremely valuable.

ARGUMENTS AGAINST BANK:

- If I calculate my salary over the time I actually invest in the job, my hourly wage is really not worth it—especially when I consider that my off hours are also being ruined by my job.

- I won't receive advancement if I don't perform and I am feeling less and less capable of even getting out of bed in the morning.

- Everything I do is mechanical and pre-ordained, I don't feel like I get to use my education.

- I don't like the people I work with.

- The experience is great *if* I want to be doing *this* for the rest of my life.

So what does this list tell us? Little to nothing—by itself. Mary's decision will depend entirely on how she evaluates each entry here. How important is long run financial success to her? How important is the extra free time the soft-money job will allow her? In the end, the list does nothing more than aid Mary in organizing her thoughts. It is not a formula for decision making, but it can provide a helpful aid. It also provides you with an opportunity to parallel pros and cons— so you see exactly what you are giving up in exchange for what you are getting.

Whether you make a list or simply evaluate the alternatives in your head, do not forget to consider all of the following areas of satisfaction/dissatisfaction:

MONEY

- How important is money for my immediate purposes?

- How important is money for my future needs?

- Is my salary more important than my time, my autonomy, my self-respect, my peace of mind?

- Can I have money and a pleasant, fulfilling job?

- Am I viewing this money question through my own eyes or someone else's? What's really going to make *me* happy? (Are you still subscribing to your parent's idea of success, are you trying to please your spouse, are you striving to meet society's notion of success at the expense of your own happiness?)

TIME

- Many people look to a job to provide them with a sense of purpose and accomplishment. Perhaps you have hobbies which bring you much more happiness but which aren't lucrative possibilities. Maybe your time away from work is more important than it is for most people. Good luck if this the case. Still, some jobs allow you to enjoy your free time more than others. Keep this in mind. Remember, the more they pay you, the more they own you.

COWORKERS

- Do you let other people's annoying habits roll right off of you or are you better off avoiding personality types which clash with yours?

BENEFITS

- Always consider salary and benefits in relationship to one another.

MISCELLANEOUS

- Where do you want to be—geographically, socially, environmentally (working environment that is)?

- Do you want to travel, do you *mind* traveling? Do you mind commuting?

- Are you considering making a decision for short term gratification that you will regret down the road?

Every situation is highly unique. For example, it may be that no amount of money is enough to keep you displaced in a heavily industrialized city in which you have already spent four months of misery and depression while longing for the more attractive scenery of home. On the other hand, you may realize that enduring just a few more months of this situation will put you in a position to relocate as you wish *and* walk away with a significantly increased salary. In such a case, the anticipated compensation would probably be enough to keep you hanging on. But few scenarios are this clear cut. Make sure you consider all of the subtle implications of the options you are considering; and, make sure you apply long and short term analysis to your considerations.

One thought to steer clear of is the idea that quitting will allow you to get even. No matter how valuable your services are, a replacement will soon follow and it is quite possible you will only be a vague memory in a few short months.

Can you ever really be sure in the *"stay or go"* decision?

I've interviewed people who tell remorsefully of a hasty decision to quit a job only to end up regretting the move for one reason or the other. Others are thankful that they had the foresight to get out of a bad situation early in the game. Quitting can be the best decision an individual makes, but it can also be a hasty and foolish act chosen without sufficient forethought, research or consideration. If quitting becomes a constant thought, you have no choice but to deal with the issue.

At times, people need to second-guess their job selection. They may, for instance, get offered another job soon after employment. Or the present job may simply prove unchallenging. As the commercial says, *"a mind is a terrible thing to waste."* In either case, controlled second-guessing is the answer.

Can I talk to anyone about my feelings?

In the office, no, absolutely not. Don't even let your actions, your facial expressions, or your tone of voice betray you. Instead, do everything in your power to keep your feelings of discontent hidden. You have nothing to gain by letting anyone know that you are considering leaving a position. What happens if you decide to stay? If your job performance should suffer at any point, colleagues *"in the know"* may interpret your wavering performance as indifference. Ordinarily, they would have allowed room for having an occasional bad day.

In fact, if you make every effort to appear to enjoy what you are doing, you may start believing the charade yourself. I am not promoting deceit. What I am promoting is a *"make the best of your situation"* demeanor. This is always the best policy. Until you have actually given notice, you don't **really** know what you are going to do. So, the safest policy is to go on as if you plan on staying with this company until retirement. Give your true feelings recognition and consideration when you are off the clock.

Companies, big and small, don't always recognize or strive to ease new grads' frustrations, but they do feel the financial impact of someone not performing up to their ability.

Until you have time to evaluate fellow co-workers, be very cautious about sharing your feelings on any company-related issues with any individual in your company. Outside contacts, such as parents, past professors, and fellow rookie 9-5ers, are a much safer source for consultation, advice, and support. Eventually, you will need to talk to someone inside the company for outsiders can do nothing to help change or correct your problems. Before signing up for classes, you sought out information about the best professors. Do the same here, seek information on who could be the best person to talk to about your feelings. Frequently, it is your immediate boss, but it never hurts to be certain.

Is there any point in voicing my complaints in the hope of working through some of my dissatisfactions?

The amount of time a company spent in recruiting and hiring you is a good indicator of how much effort they may be willing to exert to keep you. Were you hired immediately after a one hour first interview? If so, that company's efforts to help you through the 9-5 transition might be best measured in minutes. If the interview process was lengthy and detailed, then the help you receive could be the same.

Many companies invest several thousand dollars in a hiring. Don't give up too soon. The company gambled on you, and they'll give you some time to reveal results. Any relationship—even work—needs some give and take. Just don't expect to take more than you give while you're a rookie. It is not unusual for companies to have a large investment in you from day #1. As a result, it is in their best interest to see you succeed. Generally, college graduates costs companies more money than non-degreed persons, thus companies will frequently invest more time and show more patience with graduates. Is this treatment unfair to other workers? According to one employer of several graduates and non-degreed workers,

> "No, because certain people display a far greater potential. In return these people are evaluated at a different level. College grads must be looked at differently because they have no track record."

How should I relate to my boss, and vice versa?

The best place to begin with a problem is by first proving your worth and willingness to the boss. Solve any problems you can on your own. But if you can't, don't despair. Many employers will sympathize with your newness and try to encourage your continued endurance.

> *The best place to begin with a problem is by first proving your worth and willingness to the boss.*

If your boss has some interest in you, he could be a valuable counselor in dealing with your feelings about your job now and in the future. He should:

- Be interested in you as a person, not only your problems.

- Understand your positions and your duties.

- Empathize with you and make suggestions or refer you to someone who might be able to help.

- Ask you for suggestions, not just offer advice.

- Expect to see you again to see how you are doing.

- Tell you honestly when something unpleasant is just part of the job.

Mel Warriner, a director of human resources for Marriott Hotels and Resorts, says,

> *"College grads always question their decisions after 3 or 4 months. I feel there's little risk in recent graduates taking chances as long as they give any job one year to*

pan out. It takes a company and the grad some time to get to know each other."

Many new 9-5ers surveyed for this book thought their input in the work place would be as important as it was in the classroom—from the beginning. But you're not often asked to do much at the start. *"Directly, I use very little of my degree, but indirectly I use a great percentage of my education,"* tells Kristin, an '88 graduate working for the CIA. What does this mean? Kristin is indicating that although she had little opportunity to *apply* her education in the early stages of her first job, she depended on her education to understand her company's operations. Her education lay somewhat dormant while she was gaining the insight necessary to eventually put her knowledge into practice.

When some people start a job, they tend to react like a Mexican jumping bean. New grads fail to see that bosses aren't always looking for spontaneous contributions. Consider the NFL rookie. A coach who nurses him along for a season usually receives better long-term returns than one who demands results on opening day. Similarly, if your hiring hadn't been chosen for long-run results, a more experienced person would have been selected to start producing immediately.

If bosses would explain why things begin slowly—or show that they understand your impatience, it might prevent feeling so much like an alien on Planet 7.

Most graduates consider uncertainty a huge shock; veteran 9-5ers consider it a regular part of adult life. When rookies try to deny their uncertainty, they won't find satisfaction in that first job. Problems mushroom. As in every facet of life, repressing feelings of confusion only postpones what must inevitably be faced. It makes the situation harder to resolve. Though thinking out loud is considered great therapy in problem solving; it might be a very expensive session. Try to determine how much you are willing to spend.

Imagine a first job that takes you thousands of miles from home. That company has a lot of neat people who make you feel comfortable and welcome. Several months later, a competitor offers you a job at a higher salary. Is it worth jeopardizing an excellent atmosphere even for a few thousand dollars? Probably not. Those who disagree would cite the money. But you must decide what you value most.

Informing a new college hire of what to expect or what to do in case they feel dissatisfied would be very dollar wise. Employers tell employees not to hesitate to bring problems to them, and they mean it. But it's like a doctor telling you that you might have a disease and to return if you have any symptoms, without telling you what those symptoms might be. Employers often offer the *"open door,"* but fail to offer convenient opportunities for your using it.

How do bosses react to a new graduate's dilemmas?

As with any situation that involves human beings, there are a number of variables which will determine this question. Obviously, some will be more responsive and helpful than others. You are probably in a pretty good position to judge how your particular boss relates to you and your co-workers. Naturally, your use of diplomacy and tact will also determine how people relate to you.

A number of executives agreed that college graduates are simply too unsettled. One particularly opinionated veteran 9-5er expressed his attitude towards young grads quitting:

> *"Today's graduates are all messed up. Their hormones usually run wild and they place free time at too high a priority. That's a definite flaw for a good work ethic."*

Other employers are still skeptical but slightly more benevolent. Another college recruiter commented,

> *"Far too many graduates are still more dedicated to having fun than making a commitment to a job. Frankly, I don't know if I can entirely blame them. Their whole life will soon involve work. If they can afford it, let them experience something else for a time."*

If you are confident in the credibility of your complaints and you have any confidence at all in your boss's open-mindedness, go ahead and express your concerns. Explain to him that you know there are bright lights at the end of the tunnel, but how many thousand Xerox copies will you make, how many light bulbs does he expect you to change first? Be reasonable and flexible yourself. Ask for moderately challenging duties or ask only to be allowed some increased exposure to the more vital operations of your company. A deferential attitude is usually in line:

> *"I realize I am not experienced enough to take full responsibility in our more sensitive operations, but I would greatly value an opportunity to work more closely with you so as to benefit from your experience and knowledge."*

As Mel Warriner, of Marriott Hotels, says:

> *"Certain types of business cultures and environments don't encourage a recent grad to discuss their uncertainty and unhappiness. It appears that many employers expect recent grads to stumble along their way, but are ready and prepared to help if the graduate can continue to provide evidence of a prosperous future."*

Such diplomacy can never hurt. Still, you can not always count on it helping. Some people will persist in being difficult, others in being patronizing. There *are* people with whom we rational, thoughtful, and hard working people should not have to associate with. For most of us, it would take a whole lot of perks to compensate for the frustration of working with someone who can not, or refuses to, communicate and remain open to reason.

I once approached a boss with my feelings about his behavior towards me and the number of hours for which I was being paid. I had hoped my boss and the work place would change. I was partially right. The work place changed as it was soon without me.

Before spilling your guts to any boss, investigate what his reactions might be. Consider his age versus yours, how your colleagues feel about him, and what his track record has been for others with problems. A good supervisor can prevent a lot of unnecessary misery for the rookie employee if the two can create a bond of trust.

An additional factor is replacement simplicity. Can your position be filled easily or do you possess some rare traits?

If the company for which you work is established and has you in the training mode, then your boss and your job may not be the monsters you imagine them to be. They have probably seen the problems you are experiencing before. When a boss does take time out to help you, have the courtesy to try their suggestions with an open mind and patience in waiting for results. Their ideas may not work, but you have gained valuable experience in coping with future problems.

You need your job. Your boss needs you. If you're indeed a valuable asset, you can arrange some give and take. But don't be greedy, or you will definitely wind up on the short end! All give and no take is also wrong. I probably don't have to tell you that; however, you may be hesitant to stand up for your just rewards. While much of this book advises not to expect too much too soon, it is equally important not to sell yourself short.

Always keep in mind that bosses are in their position for one good reason or another. Whatever it is, take advantage of their knowledge and learn from them. Your boss is trying to keep many costly errors from occurring. Your dissatisfaction—and especially your quitting—is a reflection on him. Experiencing too many personnel losses is one error that bosses admit is costly in every aspect—their performance reviews as well as additional hiring costs.

Some bosses apparently feel the quality of your work or your answer to the simple question, *"How's everything going?"* is sufficient evidence for identifying any difficulties you have in your adjustment. Honestly, how do they expect you to answer that question? *"Well, boss, I regret the cursed day I ever set foot in this place."* Or how about, *"Well, I guess I'm alive, aren't I?"* Once you make it to the supervisory position, you should remember that specific questions always net more specific answers.

What happens if you want to quit but can't afford to do so?

Unfortunately, there might not be any alternative except sticking it out until your finances improve. If you need a steady paycheck, you need a job. Can you find some other source of income that will allow you to eke by?

Unless you're in debt over your head, avoid the *"money is everything"* philosophy. Some bosses love to have employees settled with no way out.

A Georgetown University graduate once commented on how boring a prospective job seemed and then says, *"But at that type of money you hide your imperfections and feelings of discontent."*

It's easy to understand such an attitude. Sure, you might love walking into a showroom and driving off in that BMW, but what happens when the thrill of newness is gone and you still have to go to work to pay for it?

As one discontented rookie says, *"I can quit my job, but I can't quit my car payments."*

Until you're certain about your job, refuse to be cornered by hanging a mortgage over your head or agreeing to enormous car payments—even if you could afford it. Don't paint yourself into a corner. Rent rather than buy. A Hyundai will do just as well as that BMW.

Consider the case of Bill. This manager of an electronics wholesale house had an opportunity to get a better job, but he had to decline it because he had commission checks advanced him for a major purchase. If he left, all the advanced money would have to be paid back immediately. The job possibility came and went without Bill being able to give it serious consideration.

It's wise to build up a small money reserve so that if you want to quit, you can. In the meantime, although it is impossible to conduct a full time job search *and* hold down a full-time job, you can, at least, send out resumes and try to fit in any interviews you are offered.

When is the best time to quit?

More important is selecting the time in which to contemplate quitting.

Try not to think about your job when you're extremely unhappy. In such circumstances, you can't possibly judge wisely or well.

In anything you do, remember that there are good times and bad times. Sometimes you feel great, other times just average. Don't expect to love your job every day, or use every hour to maximum efficiency.

Like class schedules, the 9-5 routine has its ups and downs. When the bad times start equaling or exceeding the good, it's time to review what you're doing.

Deciding to quit when times are bad or when you just received a poor review is going to bias your thoughts. Quitting is not a life or death drama, but it is an event that should be judged as objectively as possible.

What's the best thing to do immediately after quitting?

Once you have jumped ship, there is nothing to do but swim. If you suddenly suspect you have made the wrong decision, remember that you have nothing to gain by agonizing over it. Whatever your initial feelings about quitting, set your sights on the road ahead. Don't dwell in the past.

The agony of giving notice

When you finally decide that it's time to tell your boss, expect the worst and hope for the best. It's not an easy moment. You are risking your livelihood. Your nerves quiver. Your stomach churns. Your shirt becomes soaked. But it must be done.

Be respectful, but keep your dignity and professional attitude as well. Don't appear as the foolish and restless prodigal son. Be prepared for any objections or jabs your boss may make. Be ready with answers and replies that will reflect that you have put a great deal of thought into this decision.

Your boss will resent your move. Depending on his or her personality, s/he may take this situation as an opportunity to make you feel small and insignificant.

How you handle this situation may depend a great deal on your feelings for your boss. Maybe your boss was the one factor that made the job bearable. If so, I can think of no situations in which it would be inappropriate to say so. It may also be appropriate to point out the reasons you are leaving.

Of course, it could very well be that your boss is the primary reason you are leaving. This can make for a particularly uncomfortable situation. If you are sure you are going, you may choose to calmly and reasonably point out some of the reasons you are quitting.

In a very few cases, quitting may provide you with something of an initial high. One recent graduate, Trish Avatti, had already decided that the salary she was making in her first job was not worth the displeasure she was experiencing on the job. She felt fairly confident that she had enough contacts to do as well or better freelancing as an interior decorator. If not, she had decided that she could not be more unhappy or less financially secure working as a waitress. With this in mind, she approached her boss about a raise. When he tersely informed her that she, most assuredly would not be receiving a raise in the next few months. She responded quite calmly that, in that case, she was giving notice effective immediately. She still relishes that moment and is doing quite well on her freelance projects. But, such cases are exceptional. Only you know if you can afford to make such a bold move.

Before putting in your notice, discuss your intentions with impartial, experienced 9-5ers. A lot of valuable advice might be discovered. They may even predict what could occur and how to prepare for it. Take advantage of all available information and advice. It might make the difference between being employed and unemployed.

First, decide what you want to say. Don't ask to talk and then be vague or broad. Tell the truth, but be prudent and discreet!

Second, support, but don't exaggerate your claims. Instead of telling her you spent days doing nothing, say

> "I realize I'm only here to observe, but I spent 12 hours last week filing, and 18 hours this week. I know it's part of the territory, but I see myself doing this two months from now."

If you rehearse what you will say, with facts to back it up, your employer will have no choice but to respond to your complaints in some way. With any luck, you can set the emotional climate of the confrontation. Some people will persist in being difficult; but, you are more likely of gaining a rational response when you make a rational approach.

Third, say what you would like done. Your suggestions may not be followed, but you need to have some solutions ready for the boss. If changes won't occur, you have your decision made for you.

Grant, an '84 graduate who runs his own painting company, says,

> "College always allowed the opportunity to look back and retake an opportunity. Life after school makes recent grads accept their actions and never look back. It's all a learning experience. No matter what the outcome, it's all good experience."

After spilling the beans, you might become uncertain about your decision. It's natural to be uncertain, but don't get confused and frustrated. You decided, now do it. Personalities aside, most professionals understand a job departure.

One small business owner in south Texas explains, "*I hate losing good people, but it's part of the process. Each person has to do what they feel is best, no matter what the consequences are to a business.*"

Robert, from Princeton University, best explains:

"Many of us love our jobs, but would leave in a heartbeat if another offer was better. Loyalty is a strong deciding factor in the work place, but employers would fire employees if times turned bad."

The question of loyalty (or disloyalty) is a two way street.

Being so new in the work place might make quitting a job very dramatic. Some employers will play against your inexperience; they will try guilt trips or sympathy pleas to keep you. Do not accept such nonsense. Respond that you know no one is irreplaceable, especially you.

What's the best way to quit a job?

If possible, quit following a good business event. And, always, always, offer to allow plenty of time for replacing you.

One study indicated that the class of '87 college grads will change jobs more than ten times each in their working careers. As you will discover, quitting will be stressful. Don't make it any more so than necessary.

Often when people leave an organization, they leave wounds. Minimize the wounds, and burn as few bridges as you can. There may be a time in the future which necessitates your return or a crossing of career paths with an old colleague.

Don't forget that bosses are human too, and can be as vengeful as your worst nightmare. One worker had a dispute with his store manager. When applying for a job in the financial arena, the former employee listed his previous position as a salesman. He had, in fact, been an excellent one. But when the financial company called to confirm the information, his old boss answered and swore he was only a junior salesman.

Actions like this don't make sense, but vengeance can strike anytime, anyplace, anyone. There's nothing worse than getting hit by it. Dale Westerfeld, a grad of Baylor University and past owner of his own accounting firm, preaches, *"what goes around will eventually come around."* Dale added neither employers or employees will forget how a relationship is ended. Both must anticipate and forgive some changes, but they don't have to forget the manner in which they were treated.

If you have a good relationship with your boss, you can come to some sort of agreement—whether you stay for a standard two-week notification period or stay until a certain project is complete. It's only fair to honor a final request. Hurt feelings might be caused by your departure, but refusing a final request is like putting salt in the wound.

Try to be judged as a productive worker rather than an unproductive malcontent, even if it's only for seven more minutes or seven weeks. Why let poor behavior on those last days ruin an otherwise good record. Those last days might be your boss's final measure of you. Make it good, not bad!

If you quit a job, can you still use that employer as a reference?

It depends how you quit!

Legally, employers are not allowed to say anything that might cause you not to get another job. Consequently, employers are refusing any comment or limiting their statements to the dates in which you worked. This may seem as though it would give you a free realm to create a mess, and not have to worry about any repercussions. If the law was adhered to, that might be the case. I can't quote any statistic or fact about the percentage of employers that do restrict their comments, but be assured that a bad performance will eventually catch up to you. Considering that you are only a 9-5 rookie, and there are 40-50 year veterans, who know how to get around most rules, playing the same game. The odds are strongly against you.

When you decide to leave, try to do it with good references, even if you have to stay longer to get them. Every employer questioned agreed that a person coming to a job without references is in trouble from the start.

At the company you are departing from, leave the impression that the job move is for you and not against your co-workers or company. Exploding or blaming people for your departure is only a few fleeting moments of satisfaction which will quickly fade. It might also damage references beyond repair.

> *Leave the impression that the job move is for you and not against your co-workers or company.*

Preserve references if you're going to change jobs, but only respectable ones. Care for the people who give you references. One key is to flatter them. Inform them that deciding to leave was a very difficult decision, and could even be wrong. This statement helps release an employer from any further responsibility and guilt about failing to motivate you. Some couldn't care less, anyway. For those employers whom you leave on good terms, you might even offer them a honest critique on how their treatment of you was received. Only if they ask!

After gathering information from various sources, decide who should be a reference. The wrong references can cost you a great job. In doing a background check of you, an interested employer will change his mind if you allow bad references to speak their mind.

Some departures are nothing but negative. You are accused of A-Z. Don't retaliate. End the conversation as quick as possible and leave the premises. Will this ruin your chances for another job? Not really, but you must prove to an interviewer why there will be no references available.

Are there any special things one needs to do on their last day?

Get copies of your personnel file so that your next employer can build on your strengths and you can improve your weaknesses. If you have this, you may be able to work out a more compatible work arrangement than your previous one.

When I asked for my file at my exit interview from the bank, the senior VP said she had never had an employee ask for it before and would have to think about it for a while. I explained that I wanted to make myself a better employee. In an *"out-of-office"* settlement, we agreed to a sampling of critique sheets—confidentially, of course.

My drive to gain my full file was weakened because I was intimidated. If I had to do it again, you'd better believe I would have them before I left the building. I know now that legally, a company has no choice but to provide you with most of the information.

If gaining access to your file becomes a major problem, then go directly to your colleagues and ask for honest appraisals. Lead the individual to give you a honest appraisal. Use the *"better employee"* routine. Make them see a sincere effort on your part, or else they will return *"a candy coated"* review.

Don't give up hope if past bosses are creating havoc for you. They can make convincing others of your past work record very difficult, but not impossible. Display a very neat organized work history. If your old boss won't verify salary or that you even worked for him, show the interviewer your tax forms and give him a list of names of all those currently working there. If you have a will, there's a way.

Upon leaving a company, big or small, somewhere it is recorded whether you are eligible for rehire. Do what you can so that the *"yes"* box is checked. It is a great accomplishment to have a boss say upon leaving, *"You are welcome here anytime—you have proven your worth."*

Before quitting, make absolutely certain you have your insurance policies and any other loose ends in order. It's not true that it only happens to the *"other guy."*

For example, on the very last day of my carry-over policy coverage from one job, I was rushed to the emergency room because a lawnmower had thrown a rock into my eye. Luckily, I was covered because my mother had pestered me for three weeks to get my insurance extended. If it had expired, my savings would have died with it. The $2,000 bill would have wiped me out. Even though the very next day I started a new job with full insurance coverage, I still would have been in serious financial trouble.

It's a good idea to get all your medical needs taken care of before you venture out. Doctors don't get rich providing low-cost services. You have earned these insurance services, use them. In most states a company must extend its medical coverage.

Landlords also can ruin future departure plans. You're usually bound to a contract, but sometimes some smooth talking can change things. Prepare to lose your deposit. Be aware that a job transfer with proper documentation can legally get you out of a lease.

Get rid of as many financial commitments as you can. Make peace with your creditors: don't ignore them thinking they'll lose track of you. Keep them very informed on any changes. More times then not, they will be patient as long as you display an honest effort to satisfy your commitments. You don't want to start your new job with them calling you at work.

The more problems you solve before starting a new situation, the more time and effort you can spend concentrating on the new job.

Why do so many people second guess a decision to quit?

Take all the questions as compliments.

You may be wasting your breath when you defend your quitting. If family and friends question your intentions, be flattered, not upset. If no one cared that you're leaving, they wouldn't be pestering you. People are just concerned for your well-being and don't know how to act or what to say.

Michael, from the University of California at Santa Cruz, tells,

> *"My decisions always caused an uproar. Any new graduate has to stay confident in their own decisions. Each person knows what they can and can not do, no matter what other family members suggest."*

Potential employers are going to want to know why you quit. Try to give intelligent answers. Be able to reassure new companies that they can depend on you. Even your old company will want to understand your exit. Practice your answers on the old company to perfect them for your potential employer. It's likely that they'll ask the same questions. Know what you did and didn't learn on the job. Be able to cite all of your accomplishments and give substantial reasons for incomplete projects. (*"Incomplete"* is a key word here: never say that you failed a task!) Don't offer excuses—laggard sales, poor secretaries or malfunctioning computers—an interviewer won't be impressed.

Will the last day be weird?

Never had butterflies in your stomach before? Get ready for them your final day. You'll doubt yourself the entire day. My own feelings at that first quitting were, *"Maybe I'll tell them I've reconsidered."*

You think quitting is easy? Staying at a job you hate is the easy way. Think quitting's easy? Tell me that after you spend your first week without a paycheck. Still think it's easy? Face everyone who thinks you just can't cut it and have failed.

It's like not being able to get a date for weeks after you've broken up with your girlfriend or boyfriend. Doubts of your self worth fill your mind. You'll feel incredibly alone and constantly wonder whether or not to reunite.

Bud Carson, a senior 9-5 executive, recommends, "...*even though leaving is often an incorrect or premature decision for many new grads, if they can accept the worst possible consequences that may follow. They will be okay.*"

This is the final 9-5 shock any job can throw at you, but the worst is over. Get over your self-doubt and start building up your self-confidence. You did what you had to do. In your next job, you'll be so far ahead mentally that you'll easily overcome other shocks.

Chapter Eight

REAL WORLD SHOCKS OUTSIDE THE WORKPLACE

Along with the newness of entering the workplace, many recent grads will simultaneously experience the shock of the final severance of financial dependence upon parents. Hopefully, you began your financial weaning as a college student. Still, when you are finally cut off, your adjustment will be complicated by a fresh onslaught of previously unfathomed bills and expenses.

How much of that paycheck will I take home?

If, upon learning your starting salary, you divided that figure by the number of weeks in a year and expected to see that dividend on your weekly paycheck, you are in for a disappointment. Of course, it is unlikely that you did not realize that the government would deduct a sizeable portion for it's purposes. You probably also took into account that a designated amount would be deducted monthly to pay your portion of any group insurance policy. You may not bemoan the amount of your monthly paychecks until you have spent some time trying to meet new monthly expenses. Many new grads never considered the costs of a 9-5 job.

When an employer is courting you, the subject of money seems black and white: you'll be making more than you ever dreamed of making. The suitor company often shows you its wealth with superb perks: delicious lunches or expense-paid trips to headquarters. The corporation further feeds the impression of imminent wealth for you by always discussing its terms in pre-tax dollars and suggesting future *"bene's"* (benefits).

But when the first Friday with a paycheck rolls around, you'll see precisely what you take home. And chances are it won't go far. Work makes money, but it also requires money.

How did I manage to survive on much less as a college student?

The reasons will vary from situation to situation. However, the obvious culprit is added expenses. Some are unavoidable, others are expenses graduates may unnecessarily take upon themselves.

The high price of putting a roof over your head

At or near the top of the list of basic expenses is where you will rest your bones at night. It may seem like you live at work, but few corporations have cots and clothes closets hidden away, even for their most flagrant type A employees.

Living arrangements have some flexibility, but as a rule of thumb, figure on spending close to half of your net income on rent.

Several factors—such as size and roommates—can vary the cost, and they give you a measure of control in the housing decision. Small efficiencies exchange the discomfort of cramped space for the advantage of little maintenance. If you choose to go this rent-saving route, plan on doing most socializing outside of your fortress. Invited company may be restricted to only one or two guests unless you can convert the ironing board into a couch. But if it's clean and safe, don't complain: most of your associates have also started at the bottom.

A 1983 business graduate from Boston felt inferior at confining his abode to a room in a friend's townhouse.

> *"My boss informed me that he was finally able to rent the basement apartment he had been looking for. It dawned on me that many 9-5ers are in the same predicament."*

Alternatives and options

While you're young and relatively unencumbered, you might as well take advantage of your flexibility. Before you have accumulated a lot of *"stuff,"* why not try to continue with the scrimp and save lifestyle for a little longer. You may notice that you are happier and more carefree than peers who are anxious to prove that they have *"arrived"* before their wallets are capable of keeping up with them. Entering the working world and leaving the nest are stressful enough without multiplying your worries by accumulating bills you might avoid for a little longer.

One fantastic—if somewhat lucky—way out of the rent predicament is to find a person who wants a caretaker. Just imagine, free rent! If you can negotiate this, you might be restricted in some things, but your wallet will certainly benefit! Check with several realtors, they will be able to point you in the right direction to locate these type of arrangements.

Some people have relatives who have bought rental property for tax purposes. They don't ask much rent if they can get people who are clean, tidy and neat. Renting from friends, however, can cause problems. Keeping friends and relatives out of your business dealings is often a smart policy.

If you feel particularly creative or bohemian, you might forsake the customary apartment, townhouse, or house for other alternatives. Boats, for example, often serve as home bases to rookies living near a body of water. Boat owners are always looking for responsible individuals to watch their yachts. In the older districts of a city, you may be able to find a rear apartment converted from servants quarters or the old fashion kitchens which were once built away from the main house. In other areas of town, homeowners my offer *"in-law annexes"* for rent.

Another new twist is metropolitan real estate that doubles as rental housing by night and office space by day. God forbid if you stay out late and feel like sleeping in one morning. Well, at least you will have company for coffee.

Any sage advice for those who go the roommate route?

Know what you want and what you can tolerate, then advertise. Can you stand loud music or smokers? Don't put your patience to the test unless you absolutely must. A word of caution: the newspaper classifieds do much better at finding good places than good roommates of either gender. Roommate search services often don't help a lot, either. Some people have been very fortunate, others have had disasters. If you're new to the area and don't have much choice, be extra careful.

New graduates craving larger space usually have to give up a measure of either proximity or privacy. Choosing to save money on a dwelling *"further out"* will also increase travel time to and from work—and sitting in traffic is often worse than relaxing in a small living room. Roommates mean more space, increased capacity for entertaining, and less rent.

But roommates also mean shared responsibilities for housekeeping and yardwork—and less privacy. Just because there are more and bigger places to hide doesn't mean that they can't find you.

If you like peace and quiet as a welcome change from the office, you may find that a home with four or five others makes the workplace seem like a quiet refuge. So many areas for disagreement open up: what to watch on TV, who will wash the dishes or who needs to clean the bathroom.

Consider Dan, an '86 grad living with three other men who never liked Beethoven and still doesn't. *"The stereo is my roommate's and I have no say in the matter when he's home,"* Dan says. *"I might have roommates in the future, but I will quiz them on their musical preferences."*

Another consideration on roommates is knowing what age group you would prefer to live with. Do you work well with the elderly? Perhaps you can get a room with an elderly couple who would feel more secure with others in the house. Can you stand to live with friends, or would you rather keep the roommate relationship on a business footing? Could you live with someone of the opposite sex?

Do make sure that whomever you live with is responsible and won't be arrested for non-payment of debts or rent.

Are there any other hidden costs with getting your own place?

When you finally hit upon a place and living arrangement that suits you, there's also the matter of an initial deposit—which can range anywhere from half a month's rent to a three-month downpayment. Landlords want protection from the wild ones among you—or from those who slip away during the dead of night for parts unknown.

The rent check and deposit, of course, only get you in the door. Next you have to furnish your place unless you're a minimalist. College quarters were furnished with the unusual, the unique, the meaningful, and whatever castoffs you could scrounge.

What constitutes a *"must"* list for the unfurnished first-time residence? My recommendations include a bed (perhaps a sleeper/sofa will kill two birds with one stone), chest of drawers, lamp, something that provides music (clock radio, tape player, stereo), kitchen appliances, and a TV for Monday Night Football or whatever entertains you.

Beyond that, set your own standards. Some people just need a couch and a lamp, while others want a VCR, an answering machine, a waterbed, and a hot tub.

Just remember, the less you spend on furniture, the more you can spend on *fun*! Initial budgets rarely allow for a color television with more than four or five channels, or Waterford crystal, or Royal Doulton porcelain. And who ever said you couldn't wash plastic utensils, or use plastic ware over and over? Get what you need, at first, in any reasonable shape or color you can. Then upgrade the quality as time, money, and inclination permit.

How do you get these items if you are broke?

There are several ways to get things for your palace. Friends and relatives often have respectable furniture they no longer use. They may lend it, sell it or donate it to your cause. Failing that, check garage sales, church bazaars, pawn shops, classified ads or even the little cards tacked to grocer's bulletin boards.

Either you like shopping this way, or you don't. If you don't, prepare to go without unless you started out at $30,000 a year. If you do go bargain hunting, prepare to bargain. Just keep an eye out for hidden accessories such as bugs or molds.

Before you embark on your first furniture expedition, ask yourself how long you'll be planning to stay at your present quarters. Case in point is my wife. She requested all china for our wedding gifts. Consequently, we received an entire collection worthy of a quality cabinet. Unfortunately, our apartment did not have room for a toaster much less a china cabinet.

Most people interviewed for this book moved several times in the first years after graduation. When you've answered the duration question, gauge purchases by these yardsticks:

- What do I need?
- How hard will it be to get this to my home, and who will help?
- Will roommates/guests respect my stuff?
- Can I move out quickly if I have to?

A very conservative estimate for setting up your own living quarters is $1,500 to $2,000. Expect to pay at least $300 to $600 monthly for an apartment, as much again for a deposit, $200 for a bed, $50 for small appliances, $250 for a stereo or TV, and $100 for a used couch. If your tastes are fancy, you can easily double or triple these expenses.

Many 9-5ers go wild trying to furnish their apartments, when all they really succeed at is running up their credit limit with things they don't need.

What do landlords think of new grads?

Finally, don't rest too easy in your new quarters without knowing something about the nature of your landlord.

Many landlords unofficially demand tenants to be couples, over 27, and with no pet more obtrusive than a gold fish. This discrimination is not legal, but it will happen. Tell any landlord that you're a fresh graduate and see how you're treated. Hopefully, your foot won't be in the door when it slams.

If you don't meet the minimum, unwritten tenant standards, stock up on some Raid because the places that allow you to rent might not be worth habitation.

Whatever housemate is good at bargaining and negotiating needs to be dealing with the landlord. You can develop a good relationship if you meet the aforementioned requirements or negotiate well.

Jimmy and Renee Martin, Valparaiso University grads living in Indiana, have developed such a relationship.

Jimmy says, "*They regularly have us over for dinner and do all kinds of great stuff for us. It's much different then what I previously thought a landlord was like.*"

If you display a respect for a landlord's investment, the rewards could be very rewarding and tasty.

How come food is so expensive?

Probably because it is one of your first times that you have had to buy it. Although rent is one of the biggest new living costs, it's not the only one. Another is just as essential and even more inevitable. You might avoid rent by sleeping in a friend's closet. You might hitchhike to work to save on car expenses. But try as you might, you cannot escape the cost of food.

For many graduates this is the first time they have ever been responsible for their own meals, three times a day, 21 times a week, 84 times a month, and over 1,000 sittings a year. You might even come to miss the school cafeteria.

At a ridiculously low estimate of $2 per meal, your food bill will run over $2000 a year. That doesn't even consider snacks, dinner dates or alcohol. One recently married 9-5 couple from the University of Texas, El Paso says, "*If we can get out of Safeway under triple digits, we are happy.*" Now do you see why your mother wouldn't shop without her coupons?

Although most rookies aren't blessed with an expense account for three martini lunches, there are ways to trim food costs. Skipping meals is not one: that ultimately takes an exhausting toll on your body, wallet and Rolaids supply. Nor will your body forever subsist on the college fare of beer, peanuts and pizza. Believe it or not, in a few years the words blood pressure, cholesterol, and fat will have more meaning.

But to cut costs, if your constitution can withstand it, hit happy-hour free-food buffets. Or brown bag it to the office, requesting the pinstripe bags if necessary. Or choose from soup-and-salad bars, delis, and the ready-made sandwiches in most grocery stores. Avoid constantly eating out of vending machines: what you pay for convenience quickly adds up.

Are you starting to take better care of your clothes?

After taking care of the inner person, you must dress the outer one—and that costs more than many graduates ever anticipated. Inappropriate attire can be a serious stumbling block to one's success.

Be prepared to shop every season. For those of you who dread this task, shop smart rather than frequently. A clothes company buyer suggests that there are many short cuts that can keep a wardrobe up to par: even with refraining from buying new suits, a man can have a number of new outfits by buying new ties each season. The outcome is the same, but the expense is only a fraction of what it might be.

Continue to do your laundry regularly, keep your shoes shined, and as the buyer suggests, have more than four outfits to wear. Don't let people start making bets on what outfit you will wear today.

Getting new clothes is only the beginning of expenses—despite your pride when you saved enough money by fasting over lunch to buy them.

Did you fail to consider alterations and dry cleaning expenses? For many, this wasn't much, if any, of a college expense; now it becomes a norm. A survey of recent grads indicates that dry cleaning runs them $7 to $30 per week. Learn starches and hanging techniques if you are planning for the BMW.

Careful spending can help fit clothes with corporate culture. Some companies have a strict dress code which allows for little or no deviation in a person's personal appearance. Some Fortune 500 companies even have strict clothes color and hairstyle guidelines. Maybe the bosses all went to private school and are carrying forth the tradition of uniforms. Most of you will not have to wear the same color suit and tie, of course, but don't be the only employee wearing an all white suit.

Fit the image your boss has of you. By playing some of the *"dress for success"* game you can protect your chances of gaining all the recognition you deserve. Image can do amazing things.

When working at my first pawnshop, I gained a great deal of respect from customers because I wore a gold chain connected to a *"jeweler's loop."* Little did they know that I had no idea how to use the tool correctly. But if I took that little gold chain off, my image and credibility would have suffered greatly.

Is it shameful to live at home after graduation?

No, in fact, it seems to be growing more, instead of less, common. However, it most assuredly is not for everyone. Going back to square one has both benefits and bothers.

When debts prove too steep to manage, many graduates soon discover the familiar walls of home again. For some, it's no big deal; others can only describe it as physical and mental anguish.

"It's like a monopoly board, you go back to the start," describes one 1987 graduate from the University of Houston when asked his feelings about having to face that possibility.

The most common—and practical—advantage is saving money. Even if parents force you to pay rent, you can stash away far more substantial sums than if you lived on your own.

For one thing, as Kelly, a 1985 grad, points out, *"Living at home eliminates all those little expenses—such as light bulbs, groceries and household supplies—that you would otherwise be required to pay for."*

These *"little things"* can consume a sizable chunk of the paycheck. You never thought about the costs of a bar of soap, a light bulb, a set of curtains, a couple bath towels, a roll of aluminum foil or a gallon of milk before. They just existed, magically provided by Mom and Dad. But visit a new graduate's first residence and you may find a roll of toilet paper is not even taken for granted.

Just the joy of a well-stocked refrigerator to replace cafeteria food or the 1,000 Ways to Fix Hamburger Cookbook will justify the move home for some.

Food and supplies, of course, are only one small part of the savings. The money you can set aside at home often means the difference of whether a car payment is within your limits. It often provides the chance to gather towards the down payment on a house. For some incomes, a mortgage payment of $750 would not be an outrageous monthly expense, but raising the $10,000 to $20,000 down payment could be insurmountable if you bear the full brunt of living costs.

For those who can't begin large purchases, a more modest opportunity is simply the chance to establish credit. Most credit analysts attribute credit problems from people under age 25 to youth and inexperience. The diligent can tidy up a bleak slate.

A caveat is in order here, however: living at home will slightly weaken the credit rating of some people. Credit applications are beginning to pose the *"parent's residence"* question to prospective card holders.

Can living at home cause problems?

Security in the outside world is far less certain than it often is at home. This domestic security can be a temporary haven for those who use it wisely, but it too can be a disadvantage. Even children can wear out their welcome.

The wise way to use the security of home is to fend off the pressure of taking the first offer that comes along just for the money.

"Even with all the preliminary job search planning I did, nothing turned out for me," recalls Todd, a recent North Carolina grad who moved back home. *"If I had rent to pay, I might have been frightened into jumping at any offer."*

Eliminating such worries can produce an air of confidence you perhaps couldn't summon otherwise.

How do parents really feel about one moving back home?

Most parents agreed that today's cost of living often makes this the only choice for a new graduate. Most also admitted that there were no time restrictions in allowing such a move.

But the wise grad will set a time frame for leaving home for good. There are limits to what parents can—and should—do for you. Your move back home may restrict your parents' freedom. It might limit their ability to help other family members receive the same opportunities which you did. Just as you are different from your freshman year, so is your family. Certainly, it can be disheartening to be pressured to leave, but things could be much worse.

Put yourself in your parents' shoes. Some survived periods of tremendous economic hardship and uncertainty. They learned to be self-reliant and to understand the value of hard work and paying your own way. They want the same for you.

More often today, parents grew up in periods of prosperity. They don't always understand the intense competition of today's marketplace and see no good reason why you can't find a good job. They don't realize that an undergraduate's resume won't even get out of the personnel office in some places.

"If I can graduate in four years and immediately get a job then so can you," is an extremely popular comment from many of today's college parents according to a number of grads. *"Did our parents ever compete with 210 candidates?"* commented Joel, an '85 graduate.

> *"When I was applying for the management trainee program, I was informed that there were well over 200 applicants. And many of those were from the top schools in the country with very advanced degrees. Frankly, they were preparing me for the 'thanks but no thanks.'"*

One veteran 9-5er admitted that at the time of his graduation, a college education was often the only requirement for a good job. No longer is this always true. In today's competitive job environment an employer doesn't always swoon for a diploma. In many cases, it demands advanced degrees.

Perhaps parents have forgotten how it feels to be a recent grad looking for a profession. But perhaps our lack of years also prevents us from understanding the importance of a stable job and the real responsibility adulthood brings.

As Bunky Gallagher, mother of four recent college graduates, says

> *"Today's graduates want a lifestyle that is as good or better than that of their parents. However, many of you fail to see that it took parents more than 20 years to get there. That fact doesn't seem to matter to many grads. If you want something, you get it now. Wait isn't in the vocabulary...No one wants to refuse themselves any luxury, no matter what the consequences are."*

For certain, this debate will continue for years to come.

How do brothers and sisters react?

Many fail to understand the transitional pressures you're going through. Younger siblings tease you only because they always did, and it's fun for them. Ignore it.

Older siblings can be more complicated, particularly the already successful ones with whom you invite comparison. Keep in mind that, in time, you too will be successful.

William, a 1981 grad, says

> *"My father puts more pressure on my twin brother to succeed than anything else. I only wish he would leave him alone because he is doing more harm than good. If my brother doesn't move out of the house soon, he is going to go nuts."*

Is it normal to have weird feelings about being back home?

Comparisons and competitions are not the only pressures or disadvantages of moving back home. Some returnees feel restless and out of place, and that is normal.

Take Robbie's, a '86 graduate, situation,

> *"Christmas break was great except that my father told me that I had better have a job lined up because he wasn't going to let me bum off him again. Then he impressed upon me how much money he just laid out for my final semester of school."*

How do you react to this type of treatment? Consider Robbie's situation when you start to feel *"the living at home blues."*

"I am almost ashamed to admit it," comments one 1986 graduate, *"but I saw so many other grads getting their own place, I wondered why I had to move back home."*

Another new grad says, *"I wasn't treated badly, nor did I act negatively, but I knew living at home just wasn't right."*

Whatever you encounter, it will help to have that planned departure date and a clear sense of the goals you will accomplish by living at home for the short term. Don't waste mental energy chiding yourself as an unsuccessful, irresponsible adult. You are only capitalizing on an opportunity. Don't worry about what others think or do.

Understanding why you are living at home, be it personal or strictly financial, tends to help some individuals cope with this dependence. Reflecting on all those speeches about how graduation signifies a time to face the world on your own can cause feelings of failure. *"Oh, great,"* you might think. *"I'm real successful. An adult who can't even get out of his parent's house."* This type of self-inflicted mental agonizing is common.

It also helps to remember that other grads regret not starting out back at their parents: *"I wish I would have lived at home for my first six months following graduation. That apartment rent would have been a fair amount of savings,"* recalls Jamie, a 1987 grad. *"It would have also given me a couple months to get reacquainted with my family and friends."*

What do you do it your parents start to prohibit habits that were routine at school?

Living under parental rule often includes some sort of curfew, a restriction on party giving, and a dethroning of the *"head of household title."* If you can handle the different opinions and convictions, you've only cleared the first hurdle. What havoc occurs when you move into disapproved activity? Even the simpler, less controversial, issue of neatness can cause an uproar. At school, rooms could be a mess for entire semesters. Many college students could have been a stand-in for Oscar on *"The Odd Couple."* Most hall mates never even winked at your sloppiness as long as it was contained to your four walls. Trying to be diplomatic on this issue with parents is again a joke.

Let's conclude with a comment from one recent grad:

"Moving back home is like becoming a freshman all over again. You get to learn what's acceptable and what's not. I guess it's like pledging a fraternity. If they like you, then you can stay; if not, you've got to go."

What are all the expenses with owning a car?

Unlike food and clothes, a car can have ongoing expenses every month. Unfortunately, automobiles are almost always a necessity. Once you're all dressed up and have a place to go, you need a way to get there. Again, although college environments don't demand cars, the 9-5 workplace nearly always requires one.

Most of us would agree with Tony, a 1984 American University grad who now underwrites insurance: *"Car payments are a real pain."* Be careful that yours doesn't overextend you.

Graduation often instills new automobiles in many grads' lists of immediate wants. When the salary hits $50,000 a year, then start test driving the European sedans. Remember that your car sits in the parking lot with hundreds of others for most of the week. How much do you want to invest in a parked vehicle?

Let's say you bring home $1,200 a month. Reducing that amount by a $300 to $400 car payment is not fun. Banks and car dealerships often let new grads run greater credit risks than statistics recommend.

Claire, an '84 grad explained how she wanted a very fancy car right after graduation. She didn't get it. Two years later, after many hours of hard work in the construction management game, Claire earned the right to own her first red BMW.

Patience is often kind. All it takes is self-discipline, foresight, and hard work. The moral of Claire's story: wait and earn that dream car instead of being hasty and getting a costly second best.

Don't blink an eye if you can't afford that flashy sports car in your first year. Seek a dependable way to get to work. Transportation is your main concern. The average worker spends about $30 a week on transportation. If you can't walk to work, check all the possibilities to make sure you're using the cheapest method.

When commuting in the Washington, DC area, Barry, an '84 grad from Loyola University, used to pay $7 a day on the metro. Barry then hooked into a carpool for $5 a week. Then Barry found a community carpool pick-up point and paid just 50¢ a day—and that was to buy a newspaper. The ride to Washington was free.

So owning your own car is the answer? Only if you like making payments. A car might eliminate bus fares, but don't forget small items like gas, oil changes, and inspections. Things that can go wrong, will. One survey stated that the average car owner can anticipate spending $200 to $300 annually on unplanned car repairs alone. And let's never forget the ever antagonizing snarl known as rush-hour traffic.

Aren't credit cards a good way to establish credit?

Yes, they are also a good way to get seriously over extended. The credit card is an excellent benefit if it isn't abused. Before using this easy money, be sure of what you can afford and can't afford.

John, a '84 Texas Tech grad, says, *"What I thought was a lot of money in school really isn't. It's scary how fast your paycheck fades to nothing."*

Don, a six year 9-5 veteran, *"I remember saving $3,000 one year. After paying off my car insurance and my rent deposit, I was left with only $750. Even with more money, savings never seems to get easier."*

Nor did it help when Don received his Christmas bonus—another insurance renewal came in the mail the same day. He had enough money left for one tank of gas.

In theory, reaching a certain salary level should encourage increased savings. It rarely does. It doesn't even guarantee you won't try to live beyond your means. Take Brian from Chapter One:

> *"When I made $17,000 my first year out, I had no debt. My second year I made $22,000 and owed $3,000 to creditors. This year looks like I'll make over $40,000, but I will exceed $20,000 in money owed."*

Many 9-5ers find that they live from paycheck to paycheck while they pay back school loans and make car payments.

Easy money is alluring. One of the biggest shocks for some grads is realizing that they now have money in their wallet, or at least in a teller machine. At school, living on $20 a week was feasible. Now teller machines provide money almost anywhere, almost anytime. You no longer need schedule your spending activities around a bank's hours or wait for money to arrive in the mail.

But these machines can also jeopardize your ability to save. And credit cards, which don't monitor your checking balance for every transaction, can be even more perilous.

Those of you with little experience spending money need to know, for example, that some agencies exist solely to keep detailed records of your spending and payment habits. Finding out the contents of these credit records is seldom easy. But what they say can cause you great headaches if you give them any reason. Instead of messing with this long bureaucracy, why not keep your finances straight instead?

Weekly paychecks are supposed to produce savings, not induce havoc in your spending habits. Credit cards are too easy and can allow you to spend too much. Keep in mind you have to eventually pay the piper! The best example I remember is when I saw a young grad pay for a new suit with six different Visa cards.

Bankers must be amazed at the excuses people give for using cards instead of cash. They must laugh all the way to the bank. One favorite excuse is that a card will earn interest and cash back if you don't touch part of the money you can keep in a card account. Last month my depository interest was 63¢, and my credit card interest expense was $11.53.

Even owning a company card doesn't allow you free reign. There are many horror stories of rookies' pleading the validity of their excursions to an angry boss glaring at funny expenses on last month's expense report.

Play the credit card game safe. Controlling one card is considerably more impressive than having a wallet full of *"up to the limit"* cards.

Rationalizing that your next paycheck will get you out of debt is a first sign of credit card abuse down the road. Banks don't help curb your urges, instead they increase your card limit. Applying for 10 different credit cards on the same day will likely make you the new owner of a lot of plastic. That's what makes America great—a will to beat the system. A credit consolidator explained that having bad credit is not a barrier to getting more credit. The secret, he said, is one's persistence to continue applications for more or larger lines of credit. They eventually will be accepted. Feel this is a hazard that doesn't apply to recent grads? Then explain why so many of debt consolidators' customers are under the age of thirty. Always keep in mind that one slip in a credit record can cause years of headaches.

Before celebrating a job offer with the purchase of a new car or wardrobe, watch how making more money than ever before will be the cause for greater debt and more expenses. Having to stay at a job you hate, just so that you can pay off your Visa or MasterCard is miserable.

College emphasized freedom, the ability to question, and the desire to explore. Such freedoms dwindle with each additional purchase unless you make them all with cash. Few grads have the cash to afford the equivalent of a year's rent upfront or a new car purchase or a living room of furniture strictly in cash.

Punching a clock only to avoid creditors is a terrible way to wake up. Know what you bring home and know what you must pay out. Most important of all, know when to stop spending.

Chapter Nine

THE OTHER SIDE: SUCCESSFUL AND HAPPY

Are there new grads who have been happy from Day One?

Oh yes, there are quite a few.

If you're happy in your first job, think of your advantages: a steady lifestyle, a settled environment, a regular routine, and many benefits. Don't, however, close any doors to new opportunities. Just because you're happy, don't assume this first job is—or should be—the place where you will settle in for the next 30 years.

Believe it or not, many 9-5ers are ecstatic with their first jobs. Some did their homework and accepted jobs that would pay them well and treat them well. Some have superiors who know how to work, motivate, and discipline fresh graduates. Those 9-5ers discover that they and their companies have made solid commitments to one another. Less fortunate (and less complacent) new grads constantly wonder if a bigger pot of gold, a more fulfilling, opportunity lies hiding over another rainbow.

Are there characteristics which tend to separate the happy from the unsettled?

There are no absolute determinants. While we can observe that *"better"* students tend to get *"better jobs,"* those *"better jobs"* do not ensure contentment. Still, there is a correlative relationship between success and happiness as a scholar and success and happiness as a worker. An Arthur Young consultant, who has observed the yearly progression of new graduates through his company, observes, *"Those graduates who really hit the books in school and who are given real responsibility are very likely to be satisfied with their work position."*

There is a relationship between responsibility and happiness.

I think its important to note this observation that there is a relationship between responsibility and happiness. As indicated throughout this book, *un*happiness is often characterized, in part, by a lack of mental stimulation, a feeling of purposelessness. It should be no surprise that those who count themselves as happy are those who are given more challenging duties. In response to those veterans who have forgotten what its like to be young and full of ideas, it is not entirely fair to attribute young grads' restlessness or dissatisfaction to shiftlessness and laziness.

Recognizing the disharmonizing effect of the separation of work and purpose is no new or novel observation. Unfortunately, it is a part of modern life that the masses must learn to live with. Regardless of your feelings for his political advocations, Karl Marx had much insight into the effect of capitalism upon the human spirit. You, whether you realize it or not, continued your education in an attempt to avoid the dehumanizing condition of *"unskilled laborer."* While your most immediate incentive, or your parent's primary reason for sending you to college, was probably to increase your earning potential—you also realized the importance of gaining an education so as to live off your wits rather than your brawn.

After graduation, disillusion sets in if you find yourself performing tasks you feel you were equally prepared for four years ago—before college. If your duties hold no *meaning* for you, if you are allowed no creativity or autonomy, you will probably fall on the undesirable side of the job satisfaction fence. It's a common plight for recent grads—and often a temporary one. If you can prove your ability to accept responsibility and to act as a self-motivator early on, you may be able to avoid or quickly move past the first stages of the 9-5 shock.

What is the latest definition of success?

Where defining the components of success is concerned, there is no absolute consensus. However, I think all reasonable people would agree, a definition which does not include that elusive state of mind we call *"happiness,"* is a definition containing a contradiction in terms. Nevertheless, it seems as though many people struggle for an ill-defined conception of success without giving due consideration to the happiness factor.

For example, how valuable is money without the time or energy to enjoy it? On the other hand, I suppose you don't owe anybody any apologies if money, in and of itself, makes you feel good all over. Far be it from me to advise you to re-examine your values. Don't let others impose their definitions of success on you. It's ultimately a very personal issue.

One late night radio host claims success in the modern world means making a salary more than double your age (measured in thousands of dollars). I might venture to say there are many successful 25 year olds that are not making

$50,000 a year. Such a definition is both arbitrary and narrow. Why wouldn't a new grad making $20,000 to $40,000 a year get the Success Award? And what about all those college students who enlist in the Peace Corps? Are they not successful?

The preceding chapters have taught us, however, that satisfaction is not always guaranteed in the workplace. Some 9-5ers who claim to be happy are actually miserable, but gritting their way through, hoping for success.

Such a course of action can get you through rough patches, but be careful not to delude yourself with false reassurances for a job that can never work out. And remember that even happiness in your job doesn't exempt you from many pitfalls of the 9-5 shock.

Are there 9-5 shock relapses?

Most first jobs require both considerable thinking and considerable doing. Even if your initial transition is relatively easy, be on the alert.

A noted physical trainer once commented that the best-conditioned athletes are never more than an inch from injury. Likewise, new grads should always be aware of unexpected injuries to a career or to a career search.

If you ever think you've reached the top, don't be content to just sit there. Set new goals, perform more efficiently, do higher quality work. Don't let your drive and ambition stop.

Don't let the first grains of success and a year or two of good rapport with your firm go to your head, either. You can't insist on four weeks of vacation, instead of two. Or $50,000 instead of $20,000. Or a new home instead of a modest apartment. You will find out quickly how dispensable you still are. To expect such things early on makes about as much sense as asking to skip two grade levels in school because you aced a test or two.

Continued success depends upon your ability to use your strengths and to improve your weaknesses. If people look at you as young, remind them that youth brings flexibility and stamina. Always seek room for improvement.

Instead of waiting for the boss to tell you how you're doing, ask him to meet regularly. Keep in mind that you need your boss far more than he needs you. Be available to clarify any uncertainties or inefficiencies about your performance. Ask for criticism before it has a chance to build up.

Even the best are told that they are wrong at times. Punishment and criticism even when they do come, should be taken judiciously—especially if you've been largely successful and satisfied. Sometimes it's the old *"kick the cat"* syndrome: your boss gets an earful, and then you happen to be standing in the way.

Bosses eventually correct new employees in any number of areas—from the clothes they wear to the way they do monthly reports. As we've stressed all along, the rules and ramifications are far different than the classroom. You won't always get the gentle rebukes a kindly professor might offer.

So don't expect all smooth sailing. Strive for great things, but don't expect the workplace to be a prickle-free bed of roses. Expect aphids and thorns, and be prepared for them. Trouble can always be ahead.

For instance, one worker, who was already two years into the working world, had performed superbly representing a business supplier. But a few minutes after he closed a substantial deal from a first call to a new client, Jay's boss rang. He chastised Jay for messing up names and ignoring a regular customer. Jay's mistakes caused a large decline in other orders that month.

Little mistakes aren't job-threatening, but they can irritate your boss and impede your progress with him. Unfortunately, the 9-5 society plays by many sets of rules. Let's hope you don't enlist in a game that allows for only one strike. Accept that a successful rookie's path is bound to involve error, misunderstanding and confusion. What is one to do? Don't cry over spilt milk but sincerely demonstrate remorse and an intention to avoid repeating mistakes.

Is there a sophomore slump in the 9-5 world?

Not exactly, but becoming slack in your second year can be very dangerous.

Ron, a general manager of a Houston business, tells, *"I've given a lot of college grads their first chance, but I have also had to discipline or fire a lot of graduates for getting too big of a head and resting on their first year's performance."*

Don't forget that early career gains make you a more attractive target for corporate newcomers and political snippers. Many second year 9-5ers are awaiting their second chance to shine—at your expense, if necessary.

What's next?

More bills and higher taxes are two certainties.

At the outset of 9-5 life, contentment can be elusive for some, a fiction for others and transient for many. Unexpected setbacks will occur. Recruiters may spurn you. Interviewers can terrify you. Bosses will perplex you. Money probably won't go far enough. Housing may be hard to find. In one sense, at least, you can never go home again.

Being aware that a shock will occur is half the battle. You can never fully prepare for the 9-5 shock. It is a transition that can weigh on your soul and make you miserable for a while, but it's only a temporary condition. It won't last forever.

Christopher, a psychology graduate of Radford University, gives one possible reason why graduates experience this turmoil:

> *"It's quite harsh to make yourself accept the fact that no one is awaiting your arrival. I finally told myself that there were 9 million other graduates out there. Graduation might have led you to have big dreams, but you'd better wake up real fast. College simply isn't the real world and work is."*

But these shocks might just help graduates mature in the business world. That's part of the reason the veterans who work with you—and over you—allow it.

Confidence in yourself and the knowledge that you're not alone in this predicament are really the only weapons you need. Put another way, you are not in this boat alone. Nor is it about to capsize. You may founder; you need not drown. Nobody is singling you out for special misery. Bide your time, even if a few storm waves rise suddenly, buffet you, and leave you momentarily breathless or sputtering. Things will almost certainly get better. In your efforts to change things for the best, you will have conquered the first challenge.

Don't indulge in panic. Many of those interviewed for this book are now prospering. I even overcame the 9-5 Shock, but I paid the price. Forty plus interviews, one year at a bank, two years at a pawnshop, eight weeks in the military, two weeks in the insurance business, one year as a door-to-door salesman, three months as a waiter, and four weeks as a warehouse clerk are just several samples of my dues. Now, I am running a segment of a company where I make almost all my own decisions. My pay is more than double my age and I also have an expense account. I do consider my self moderately successful, but like so many of the happy graduates that I interviewed attested, it wasn't easy getting here.

The workplace and its shocks await you. But now you are better prepared to anticipate this eventful experience. So sit back and enjoy the trip. After all, you'll probably be on it, 9-5, for the next 40 years!

INDEX

A
Achievement, 104
Acquaintances, 65-70
Adjustments, 16-17, 19
Alumni, 72-73
Answers, 81-85
Applicants, 81-82
Attitudes, 116
Authority, 24

B
Benefits, 43-49
Bosses, 21-22, 123-126, 140-145, 179

C
Car, 170-172
Career change, 132
Career placement offices, 70-71
Classroom, 2
Clothes, 164-165
College, 4
Complaints, 139
Conformity, 20
Connections, 58
Contacts, 61-77
Cooperation, 118
Costs, 157-165
Creativity, 20
Credit, 172-174
Criticism, 179
Culture, 1

D
Deadlines, 111-113
Decision-making, 38-39
Degrees:
 college, 13
 value of, 6, 9

Details, 100
Diplomacy, 143

E
Employers:
 attitudes, 103
 expectations, 36, 79, 123-124
 fears, 51
 hiring, 59
 needs, 37
 questions, 85-86
Expectations, 2-3
Experience, 87-89
Extracurricular activities, 115-116

F
Fatigue, 23
Food, 163
Frustrations, 7, 12

G
Giving notice, 146-147
Gossip, 76, 103-107
Graduates, 11-12

H
Happiness, 175-181
Hiring, 103, 139
Hours, 25
Housing, 157-161, 165-170

I
Impressions, 99-101
Insurance, 45-46
Interviews, 78-101

J
Jealousy, 76

183

Job:
  first, 13-14, 29-32, 38
  frustrations, 5, 32
  normal, 29
  offers, 93-95
  preparation, 8
Job search:
  considerations, 41-42
  organization, 52-77

L
Landlords, 162-163
Last day, 152--153
Listening, 64

M
Mistakes, 113-115, 179
Money, 42-44

N
9-5 shock:
  defined, 6-8
  responsibility, 10
Networking, 58-77, 98
Noticed, 110

O
Obedience, 116-118
Organizations, 21

P
Parents, 165-170
Patience, 120-123
Paychecks, 156-157
Performance, 24
Personnel file, 152
Play, 118
Politics, 23, 103-105
Preparation, 5
Pressures, 24
Professional organizations, 72
Professionalism, 100
Professors, 71-72
Profit sharing, 47
Punctuality, 89

Q
Questions, 80, 85-86, 89-92
Quitting, 127-138, 145-155

R
Realities:
  college, 15
  workplace, 2
Reciprocity, 73-75
Rejections, 66
Relocation, 49-50
Responsibility, 176
Restlessness, 36
Resumes, 52-58
Roommates, 159-160

S
Salaries:
  starting, 42-43
  structure, 45
Self-reliance, 20
Shocks, 6-7
Skills, 3-4
Small talk, 64
Success, 175-181

T
Taxes, 45
Team play, 27-29
Time:
  starting, 35
  work, 24-26, 111-113

V
Vacations, 46-47

W
Workplace:
  characteristics of, 22-25
  perceptions of, 4
  survival rules, 20
  values, 20

CAREER RESOURCES

The following career resources are available directly from Impact Publications. Complete the following form or list the titles, include postage (see formula at the end), enclose payment, and send your order to:

IMPACT PUBLICATIONS
4580 Sunshine Court
Woodbridge, VA 22192
Tel. 703/361-7300
FAX 703/335-9486

Orders from individuals must be prepaid by check, moneyorder, Visa or MasterCard number. We accept telephone and FAX orders with a Visa or MasterCard number.

Qty.	TITLES	Price	TOTAL

CAREER TRANSITIONS

___	Careering and Re-Careering For the 1990s	$13.95	___
___	From Campus To Corporation	$10.95	___
___	Graduating To the 9-5 World	$11.95	___
___	Starting Over	$11.95	___
___	Transitions	$10.95	___

JOB SEARCH STRATEGIES AND TACTICS

___	Complete Job Search Handbook	$12.95	___
___	Go Hire Yourself An Employer	$9.95	___
___	Joyce Lane Kennedy's Career Book	$29.95	___

___ The Right Place At the Right Time $11.95 ___
___ Super Job Search $24.95 ___
___ Wishcraft $7.95 ___
___ Who's Hiring Who $10.95 ___

SKILLS IDENTIFICATION, TESTING, AND SELF-ASSESSMENT

___ Career Sort Assessment Instruments $23.95 ___
___ CareerMap $12.95 ___
___ Charting Your Goals $12.95 ___
___ Discover the Right Job For You! $11.95 ___
___ Discover What You're Best At $10.95 ___
___ Quick Job Hunting Map $3.95 ___
___ The Real-Life Aptitude Test $10.95 ___
___ The Three Boxes of Life $14.95 ___
___ The Truth About You $11.95 ___
___ What Color Is Your Parachute? $11.95 ___
___ Where Do I Go From Here With My Life? $11.95 ___

RESEARCH ON JOBS, ORGANIZATIONS, CITIES, AND FIELDS

___ 101 Careers $12.95 ___
___ American Almanac of Jobs and Salaries $15.95 ___
___ America's Phone Book $24.95 ___
___ California $9.95 ___
___ Career Finder $14.95 ___
___ Careers Encyclopedia $29.95 ___
___ Dictionary of Occupational Titles $32.95 ___
___ Directory of Executive Recruiters (1991) $39.95 ___
___ Encyclopedia of Careers and
    Vocational Guidance $129.95 ___
___ Enhanced Guide For
    Occupational Exploration $29.95 ___
___ Exploring Careers $19.95 ___
___ Guide to Occupational Exploration $36.95 ___
___ Hoover Handbook: Profiles of Over 500
    Major Corporations $19.95 ___
___ *"How To Be Happily Employed in..."*
    Boston, Dallas/Ft. Worth, San Francisco,
    Washington, DC ($10.95 each or $42.95
    for set of 4) $42.95 ___
___ *"How To Get a Job in..."* Atlanta, Chicago,
    Dallas/Ft. Worth, Houston, Los Angeles/
    San Diego, New York, San Francisco,
    Seattle/Portland, Washington, DC ($15.95

Career Resources

each or $139.95 for set of 9)	$139.95 _____
___ *Job Bank Series:* Atlanta, Boston, Chicago, Dallas, Denver, Detroit, Florida, Houston, Los Angeles, Minneapolis, New York, Ohio, Philadelphia, Phoenix, San Francisco, Seattle, St. Louis, Washington, DC ($12.95 each or $229.95 for set of 18)	$229.95 _____
___ Job Hunter's Sourcebook	$49.95 _____
___ Jobs! What They Are, Where They Are...	$11.95 _____
___ Jobs 1991	$14.95 _____
___ Jobs Rated Almanac	$14.95 _____
___ L.A. Job Market Handbook	$15.95 _____
___ National Trade and Professional Associations	$59.95 _____
___ Occupational Outlook Handbook	$17.76 _____
___ Places Rated Almanac	$16.95 _____
___ Professional Careers Sourcebook	$69.95 _____
___ Top Professionals	$10.95 _____

RESUMES, LETTERS, AND NETWORKING

___ 200 Letters For Job Hunters	$14.95 _____
___ Damn Good Resume Guide	$7.95 _____
___ Does Your Resume Wear Blue Jeans?	$7.95 _____
___ Dynamite Cover Letters	$9.95 _____
___ Dynamite Resumes	$9.95 _____
___ Great Connections	$11.95 _____
___ High Impact Resumes and Letters	$12.95 _____
___ How To Work a Room	$8.95 _____
___ Is Your *"Net"* Working?	$22.95 _____
___ Network Your Way To Job and Career Success	$11.95 _____
___ Perfect Cover Letter	$9.95 _____
___ Perfect Resume	$10.95 _____
___ Resume Catalog	$13.95 _____
___ Resumes That Knock 'Em Dead	$7.95 _____
___ Sure-Hire Resumes	$14.95 _____
___ Your First Resume	$10.95 _____

DRESS, APPEARANCE, AND IMAGE

___ Dress For Success	$10.95 _____
___ Dressing Smart	$19.95 _____
___ Professional Image	$10.95 _____
___ New Etiquette	$14.95 _____
___ Secret Language of Success	$18.95 _____
___ Women's Dress For Success	$8.95 _____
___ Working Wardrobe	$11.95 _____

INTERVIEWS AND SALARY NEGOTIATIONS

____ Dynamite Answers To Interview Questions	$9.95	_____
____ Five Minute Interview	$12.95	_____
____ How To Get Interviews From Job Ads	$16.95	_____
____ How To Make $1,000 a Minute	$7.95	_____
____ Interview For Success	$11.95	_____
____ Power Interviews	$12.95	_____
____ Salary Success	$11.95	_____
____ Sweaty Palms	$8.95	_____

PUBLIC-ORIENTED CAREERS

____ 171 Reference Book	$18.95	_____
____ American Almanac of Government Jobs and Careers	$14.95	_____
____ Compleat Guide To Finding Jobs in Government	$14.95	_____
____ Complete Guide To Public Employment	$15.95	_____
____ Find a Federal Job Fast!	$9.95	_____
____ How To Get a Federal Job	$15.00	_____
____ Jobs and Careers With Nonprofit Organizations	$13.95	_____
____ Profitable Careers In Nonprofit	$12.95	_____
____ Right SF-171 Writer	$14.95	_____

INTERNATIONAL AND OVERSEAS JOBS

____ Almanac of International Jobs and Careers	$14.95	_____
____ Complete Guide To International Jobs and Careers	$13.95	_____
____ Guide To Careers In World Affairs	$11.95	_____
____ How To Get a Job In Europe	$15.95	_____
____ International Careers	$11.95	_____
____ International Consultant	$22.95	_____
____ International Jobs	$12.95	_____
____ Passport To Overseas Employment	$14.95	_____
____ Work, Study, Travel Abroad	$11.95	_____

MILITARY

____ Does Your Resume Wear Combat Boots?	$7.95	_____
____ Re-Entry	$13.95	_____
____ Retiring From the Military	$22.95	_____
____ Woman's Guide To Military Service	$10.95	_____
____ Young Person's Guide To the Military	$9.95	_____

EDUCATORS

___ Alternative Careers For Teachers $8.95 _____
___ Careers In Education $16.95 _____
___ Educator's Guide To Alternative
    Jobs and Careers $13.95 _____

WOMEN AND SPOUSES

___ Best Companies For Women $9.95 _____
___ Careers For Women Without College $10.95 _____
___ Female Advantage $19.95 _____
___ Relocating Spouse's Guide To Employment $12.95 _____
___ Women Changing Work $12.95 _____

COLLEGE STUDENTS

___ College Majors and Careers $15.95 _____
___ How You Really Get Hired $8.95 _____
___ Internships $27.95 _____
___ Liberal Arts Jobs $11.95 _____
___ Put Your Degree To Work $9.95 _____

JOB LISTINGS AND NEWSLETTERS

___ Career Planning & Adult
    Development Newsletters (6 issues) $30.00 _____
___ Career Opportunities News (6 issues) $30.00 _____
___ Federal Career Opportunities (6 issues) $37.00 _____
___ Federal Jobs Digest (6 issues) $29.00 _____
___ International Employment Gazette (6 issues) $35.00 _____
___ International Employment Hotline (12 issues) $39.00 _____

CHILDREN, YOUTH, AND SUMMER JOBS

___ A Real Job For You $9.95 _____
___ Teenager's Guide To
    the Best Summer Opportunities $9.95 _____

MINORITIES AND IMMIGRANTS

___ Black Woman's Career Guide $14.95 _____
___ Directory of Special Programs For
    Minority Group Members $31.95 _____
___ Finding A Job In the U.S. $7.95 _____
___ The Minority Career Book $9.95 _____

EXPERIENCED AND ELDERLY

____ 40+ Job Hunting Guide	$23.95	____
____ Getting a Job After 50	$29.95	____

ALTERNATIVE CAREER FIELDS AND ENTREPRENEURSHIP

____ Best Jobs For the 1990s . . . and Into the 20th Century	$12.95	____
____ *"Career Choices for the 90s"* Series (all 12 titles)	$99.95	____
____ • Art	$8.95	____
____ • Business	$8.95	____
____ • Communications/Journalism	$8.95	____
____ • Computer Science	$8.95	____
____ • Economics	$8.95	____
____ • English	$8.95	____
____ • History	$8.95	____
____ • Law	$8.95	____
____ • Mathematics	$8.95	____
____ • MBA	$8.95	____
____ • Political Science/Government	$8.95	____
____ • Psychology	$8.95	____
____ *Career Directory Series* (all 8 titles)	$157.95	____
____ • Advertising	$19.95	____
____ • Book Publishing	$19.95	____
____ • Business & Finance	$19.95	____
____ • Magazine Publishing	$19.95	____
____ • Marketing	$19.95	____
____ • Newspaper Publishing	$19.95	____
____ • Public Relations	$19.95	____
____ • Travel & Hospitality	$19.95	____
____ *"Career Opportunities in..."* Series (all 4 titles)	$137.95	____
____ • Art	$27.95	____
____ • Music Industry	$27.95	____
____ • TV, Cable, and Video	$27.95	____
____ • Writing	$27.95	____
____ *"Careers in..."* Series (all 8 titles)	$132.95	____
____ • Careers In Accounting	$16.95	____
____ • Careers In Business	$16.95	____
____ • Careers In Communications	$16.95	____
____ • Careers In Computers	$16.95	____
____ • Careers In Education	$16.95	____
____ • Careers In Engineering	$16.95	____
____ • Careers In Health Care	$16.95	____

____ • Careers In Science	$16.95	____
____ Careers With Robots	$26.95	____
____ Flying High In Travel	$14.95	____
____ How to Become a Successful Consultant	$19.95	____
____ Job Opportunities For Business & Liberal Arts Graduates	$19.95	____
____ Job Opportunities For Engineering, Science, and Computer Graduates	$19.95	____
____ Jobs For People Who Love Travel	$11.95	____
____ Making It In the Media Professions	$18.95	____
____ New Accountant Careers	$13.95	____
____ *"Opportunities in..."* Series (140+ titles: $12.95 each or $1849.95 for set; contact publisher)	$1849.95	____
____ Outdoor Career Guide	$23.95	____
____ Planning Your Medical Career	$17.95	____

                    SUBTOTAL   ____

Virginia residents add 4½% sales tax   ____

POSTAGE/HANDLING ($3.00 for first title and $.50 for each additional book) $3.00

TOTAL ENCLOSED ------------------- ____